The Soul

Rabbi Adin Even-Israel
Steinsaltz

The Soul

Steinsaltz Center
Maggid Books

The Soul
First English Edition, 2018

Maggid Books
An imprint of Koren Publishers Jerusalem Ltd.

POB 8531, New Milford, CT 06776-8531, USA
& POB 4044, Jerusalem 9104001, Israel
www.maggidbooks.com

Original Hebrew Edition © Adin Even-Israel Steinsaltz, 2015

English Translation © Adin Even-Israel Steinsaltz, 2018

This book was published in cooperation with the Steinsaltz Center
and/or the Israeli Institute for Talmudic Publication. All rights
reserved for Rabbi Adin Even-Israel Steinsaltz and Milta Ltd.

ISBN 978-1-59264-476-6, *hardcover*

A CIP catalogue record for this title is
available from the British Library

Printed and bound in the United States

*We dedicate this wonderful book in honor of our forefathers
and our ancestors with the desire that our descendants
continue our family legacy: be true to our Jewish values,
be humble and charitable, and always lead by example.*

Alberto and Gay Peisach

Contents

Foreword

HAVE YOU ENCOUNTERED your soul yet? Are you paying attention to your soul?

When a secular entrepreneur has the rare opportunity to have a close encounter with a giant talmudic scholar, a Torah master, and an evolved soul seeker of the stature of Rabbi Adin Steinsaltz, a new dimension opens. No magical lights, no sounds, no fireworks, no epiphany, no revelations, and at first no conscious transformation; but a door to the Infinite opens from the subtle soft voice transcending all physical dimensions from above to below as one experiences a soul-to-soul encounter.

For some reason unbeknownst to me, it was my destiny to meet and get to know Rabbi Adin Steinsaltz. In one of our many meetings, I saw that Rabbi Steinsaltz was tired from his work and there was still a room full of people waiting to meet with him. I asked him, "Rabbi, you have so many things to do, lectures to give, books to write…. Why do you spend the time talking to me?" He looked at me with his deep, penetrating blue eyes and profoundly said, "Because you listen."

The Rabbi explains that "people run around a lot, not in order to get to any particular place, but mainly to escape from themselves. But, in fact, a person should pay attention to the anguish of his soul, however it manifests itself. ..."

I feel privileged to have had the opportunity to work on and discuss *The Soul* with Rabbi Steinsaltz. If we want to evolve as human beings, we need to assume the responsibility of acknowledging our soul, to distinguish our actions from reactions and behave accordingly. Listen to your soul.

Alberto Peisach

Part I

About the Soul

IT IS UNCLEAR how early in life we discover that we have a soul. Nevertheless, the soul is one of the first things we do perceive, even if we don't perceive it fully. This is similar to our perception of our bodies, which also develops in stages. As children, we probably discovered our stomachs because there was sometimes pain there, for example. Then, through the senses of sight and touch, we gradually discovered our hands, feet, and other body parts, until we came to a full awareness of our bodies. As adults, we conduct a constant, loving dialogue with the body (possibly too loving!) and are always dealing with it and caring for it to some degree. Nevertheless, more of it is hidden from us than perceived by us. While we are able to see and touch the external parts of our bodies, we are not so intimately acquainted with our internal organs and systems, whose workings are hidden.

Likewise, the experience of the soul does not enter our consciousness as a complete, unified perception. It penetrates our consciousness as an accumulation of experiences: love and hate, attraction and abhorrence, curiosity and learning, and so on. These experiences appear individually. Only at a later stage do they accumulate and form some sense of Self.

When the totality of these experiences is finally perceived by us as the Self, even an unsophisticated person can differentiate between self in the physical sense and Self in the spiritual sense, which is a part of the soul. Our acquaintance with the soul is fundamental, and we are aware of it long before we can give it a name. However, just as our acquaintance with our bodies begins with externally focused perceptions, our acquaintance with our souls also begins with externally focused experiences, while its inner workings are far less apparent.

So the soul is something we sense. We are as certain of its existence as we are of the body's existence, but we don't know much about it.

Throughout the ages, attempts have been made to define the soul – not only to define it, but also to locate it. The Greeks thought the locus of the soul was the diaphragm. By contrast, the Torah states that "the blood is the soul" (Deuteronomy 12:23). This perception is perhaps related to the idea that the heart is the basis of physical existence as well as the focal point of the soul. All of these efforts are attempts to resolve the enigma of the soul by locating it somewhere in the body.

After many generations of observation, it is generally accepted that the soul is located in the brain. However, scientists and philosophers, as well as other thinking people, know that this sort of definition is merely convenient shorthand and not really a description. Even those who locate the soul in the heart or brain know that these organs are pieces of flesh. They are, at best, points of contact with the soul, but do not constitute the soul itself.

While there is an essential perception of Self within the soul, this perception has no content; it is merely a declaration. In other words, our acquaintance with our souls is essentially no different from our acquaintance with other people. We might know what clothes they wear, what they look like, or even their way of thinking. Nevertheless, they are still foreign to us. They are familiar to us only through their extrinsic features, not their inner content. A person's mind contains millions of details, most of which are unknown to anyone else and are unlikely to ever become known to anyone else. But the awareness of Self is beyond these details. "I know," "I think," "I feel," and even "I am alive" are manifestations of self-awareness. But they cannot bring us closer to real familiarity with our souls.

Some people are inclined to contemplate the essence of their souls. Others can live their entire lives – even lives of intellectual activity – without taking an interest in their souls at all. These different attitudes are influenced by personality certainly, but also by our inner world of experiences. Those whose lives are externally centered do not give their own souls much thought. The more we are aware of inner experiences – such as love and hate, hope and despair – the greater the chance that these experiences will awaken some sort of awareness of the full depth and breadth of our souls. But even people who are self-aware – who spend at least some time thinking about their souls – do not usually reach beyond the scope of their existing experiences.

So while every person has a soul, the soul eludes definition. The Maharal[1] puts it like this: "In one way or another, we all sense our soul and know that it exists, yet we do not know what it really is." It is specifically those who spend time exploring the soul who understand that although they are familiar with the layers and parts of the soul, and even with its functions, they are still unable

---

1. Judah Loew ben Bezalel, widely known as the Maharal of Prague, was an important sixteenth-century talmudic scholar, Jewish mystic, and philosopher. This comment appears in the introduction to his work *Gevurot Hashem*.

to perceive its essence. They are aware that they are dealing with superficial manifestations of its existence and not with its ultimate nature. It has been said of God that He is "the closest being and yet the most distant being."[2] So, too, the soul.

These and other mysteries that dwell beyond intellectual consciousness have been revealed to only a few individuals over the course of time. These few are the ones who can speak of the essence of a soul. The content of this book draws on the illumination of, and is written in the spirit of, those true masters of the soul – certain great sages who were aware of their divine souls and were intimately connected to them. Having been party to such knowledge, they have conveyed some of its mysteries and have revealed parts of its essence to us.

---

2. Rabbeinu Baḥya ben R. Yosef Ibn Pekuda, *Ḥovot HaLevavot, Sha'ar HaYiḥud*, chap. 10. Rabbeinu Baḥya was a medieval Jewish philosopher.

What Is the Soul?

W E HAVE SEEN that it is impossible to pin down the soul. Yet, if we wish to speak about it, we need a common understanding of what we are talking about. Language, though imperfect, is the only tool available to us for this purpose. Whatever vocabulary or terminology we choose is certain to create a particular image of the soul. Such an image can be useful in moving us ever closer to some understanding of the soul. But it is only an image. Thus, in the chapters ahead, we will not confine ourselves to a single image. To do so would imply that the soul actually can be confined in this way – or confined at all. Instead, we may use different language in different contexts, which will conjure different imagery in different chapters, or sometimes in the same chapter.

To begin, then:

The soul is, of course, immaterial, and it is not only beyond matter but also beyond what is considered spirit: that is, it is beyond whatever the intellect, at its highest, can reach and understand or make clear to itself. The soul is thus not to be conceived as a certain defined entity, caged in the body, or occupying a finite space. Instead, it should be thought of as a continuous line of spiritual being, stretching from the primary source of all the souls to beyond the specific body of a particular person. When we speak of the primary source, the foundation of that ineffable presence that is the soul, we can say that all souls emanate from a single point; all souls are like reflections of one source of light on different objects. While each soul is a singularity unto itself, the light of the primary source exists within it, too. We could say, then, that all souls come from the same source, all souls have the same value, and all souls exist on the same level. However, when souls descend to the world from this primordial source, and even more so when they become manifest in the reality of our world – in other words, when they come to dwell in human bodies – they are no longer equal. What is more, no two souls are identical. Every soul is unique; each soul has its own essence and character that is different from those of any other soul.

The soul, then, in relation to the entirety of life, is like the vital force that animates everything in existence. This energy is not something we may take or leave; it is an inner reality. It is what germinates the seed of the fruit and causes the tree to grow. It lies at the foundation of every living being.

According to Jewish mystical literature, there are several levels of the soul, and they are parallel to levels in the spiritual universe in general. In the language of the Kabbalah, the *nefesh* level corresponds to our world, which is called the "world of action"; the *ruaḥ* level corresponds to the "world of formation"; and the *neshama* level corresponds to the "world of creation." Because these worlds, despite their differences, are in a certain sense a single unit, the levels *nefesh, ruaḥ,* and *neshama,* although distinct, are located on a single continuum.

The higher level of the soul, the *ḥayya* level, essentially corresponds to the world of *atzilut,* or proximity to God, which is not exactly a world but a type of divine revelation. Therefore, people seldom discover this level, and when they do, it is only thanks to tremendous effort on their part, which enables them to ascend and reach some sort of connection with the divine revelation. The highest level, the level of *yeḥida*, is beyond even the world of *atzilut*, and in a certain sense, it is not part of the soul of a specific individual but is included in the primary source of all souls. This is why it is called *yeḥida*, singular, as it is the single, general soul that is shared by all. Throughout the generations, there have been only a few individuals, called "masters of the *ḥai*" (an acronym for *ḥayya-yeḥida*), who achieved enlightenment on the level of *ḥayya-yeḥida*, essentially setting themselves apart from other human beings.

It is possible for human beings to ascend from one level to a higher one, but it is a task involving great exertion. In fact, our spiritual personas can be likened to a multistory building where the first, lowest floor in the building is the *nefesh* level, above it is the *ruaḥ* level, and above that is the *neshama* level. Above that is the lofty level of the soul called *ḥayya*, and above this is the ultimate level called *yeḥida*. All of these levels exist within everyone! However, some of them are accessed only by certain individuals. Most of us dwell on the ground floor of this multistory building, the *nefesh* level, and do not necessarily occupy that floor fully. We start to ascend when our awareness of our inner selves does not remain at the first level but starts to rise. While success in making this ascension is due, in some measure, to the grace of God or our God-given gifts, it depends first and foremost on our own conscious decision to attempt the climb. But even if most people choose to remain on the ground floor – and there are those who actually prefer the basement – the entire building is open to anyone who makes the effort.

For our purposes here, we are interested in two levels of the soul: the *nefesh* (the vital soul) and the *neshama* (the godly soul).[1] At the most basic level, everything in the animal and mineral world has a *nefesh*. For human beings, as we have seen, the *nefesh* is the lowest level of our non-material existence (thoughts, feelings, etc.), and we are in constant contact with it. But unlike the *nefesh*, which includes many components related to both the physical and the spiritual sides of life, the main characteristic of a *neshama*, a soul, any soul, is that it is a spark of God. This is why the entirety of the soul's existence is impelled toward its Creator.

From another perspective, we can say that the difference between the *nefesh* and the *neshama* lies in their foundations and their basic inclinations. The *nefesh* is the Self, the more conscious part of our inner being, and it works within every person to fulfill the needs and desires of the Self, whether they are physical and instinctive or abstract and spiritual. (More about the Self in the next chapter.)

The *neshama*, on the other hand, is not driven by the Self, but exists beyond the Self. It has no physical anchor; it is spiritual and abstract. It is not directly involved with the human body; it is involved with sanctity and with the human relationship with God. It connects with the human Self through the *nefesh*.

It follows that, in a certain sense, these two components of the soul – the *nefesh* and the *neshama* – are one, or are at least located on the same continuum. But in another sense, they are distinct. For this reason, human beings hold within them an inherent duality: two souls that act as one but on two different paths. At times, the fundamental differences between the impulses of

---

1. In the imagery of the Kabbalah, the level of the soul that includes the *nefesh*, *ruah*, and *neshama* demands the presence of all three. For our narrative, however, the focus is on the *nefesh* and/or the *neshama*, but not the *ruah*.

these two parts of the soul lead them to conflict. What's more, the interaction between them is constantly influencing our thoughts, speech, and actions. And since these two souls act as one more often than not, we do not always perceive them as distinct from one another. Therefore, we do not know the source of every thought or urge we have. Indeed, a large part of our spiritual development is learning to distinguish these different components – the vital soul (*nefesh*) and the godly soul (*neshama*) – and hearing how each addresses us individually and how they address us as one.

The Manifest Soul

So far, we have discussed the nature of the soul, how we tend to conceptualize it, and the images we use to speak about it. We have also looked into that strange part of our soul called the Self. But how do you know your own soul? How do you recognize it? Interact with it? Can you call it forth? Or does it call you forth? Let's take a closer look.

Whether, when, and how a soul manifests itself depends on a few things. Education and cultural environment are chief among them. Education is not just transferring information or training children to behave in a certain way; it also involves transmitting customs and traditions, rules and mores (consciously or unconsciously). This is true in every society, past and present. In some societies, education is well defined and stable, and it may include spiritual elements if the society wishes to emphasize those; in others, not. Belief in God can be a personal matter, or it can be common to an entire society. It can be expressed in a private way, or it can be expressed within an organized, ceremonial, ritual structure. In all cases, it takes form according to the nature of the cultural environment. Here, as elsewhere, the influence of education, at home or in an educational institution, is either weakened or strengthened by the environment. A supportive cultural environment will reinforce basic education, while a non-supportive or hostile society will weaken the education's effect or even erase it completely.

At times during the course of history, spiritual and religious matters were emphasized and encouraged in homes and in religious and educational institutions everywhere. In such an environment, an individual soul would be likely to manifest and to flourish. By contrast, during periods of history when religion or spirituality were out of fashion, just the opposite would be likely: individual souls would not be so inclined to manifest or flourish. The same was – and continues to be – true on a local level. If we were to examine a particular geographical area at any particular time in history, we would probably find the same phenomenon. Some cities or towns or neighborhoods would encourage – through culture and education – the development of the soul. In such circumstances, people would likely discover their souls at a young age and perceive them in a clear way. Other cities, towns, or neighborhoods in the same area would fail to even acknowledge the soul, with an equally predictable outcome.

There are a few wild cards in this formula, however, and one of them is heredity. There are various capabilities that are part of our genetic makeup, but not all of them emerge organically; some require education and cultivation to be brought to fruition. This reality can be likened to various capabilities that most people possess but that become apparent only under suitable conditions. For example, most people have the ability to learn how to read and write. Experience shows that this capability exists even among people who were raised in cultures that never developed an alphabet, and consequently never had the chance to express the ability to read and write. However, a child from such a culture who is placed in a school will learn how to read and write in exactly the same way that a child born into a culture possessing an alphabet will learn.

Another departure from the rule involves those unusual people who succeed in expressing their abilities even in surroundings completely lacking the necessary framework for doing so. The souls of such exceptional people will be illuminated within them so clearly that they are compelled to discover them, even in the absence of the appropriate environmental conditions.

A second important influence on how the soul manifests is the level of the soul itself. A high soul is also a clear, strong soul, and whoever has such a soul is more strongly aware of it than someone whose soul is small or low. The distinction between a great, or high, soul and a small, or low, soul does not have to do with talent, and certainly not with actions. The level of the soul is simply a trait that exists within each of us. There are people whose great souls will be revealed in everything they do, in their breadth of vision, in the loftiness of their desires, in their ability to perceive hidden spiritual heights. At root, the difference between high and low souls is the difference between those whose souls are based on expansive vision and lofty goals and those whose desires and horizons are narrow and confined. These differences are unrelated to anything that can be explained in terms of material existence. God distributes souls in a manner that seems arbitrary to us.

Although we do not choose our souls or the way they reveal themselves, all of us are capable of discovering more noble elements within ourselves. There is inner work to be done, however, and this is important: we must access the higher levels of our souls and cause them to manifest within our active consciousness. All of the levels of the soul exist within every person. By accessing the higher levels, we are able to liberate ourselves from the assumptions of a particular culture, or the assumptions of the point in history we happen to be living in.

The vehicle through which our souls are manifest is usually an epiphany of some kind, beyond time, place, culture, or level of the soul. An epiphany can be thought of as a sudden insight of great importance that seems to come out of the blue. But not all epiphanies are the same. They differ in nature and effect from person to person. They can also differ within the lifetime of a single person.

For instance, most of us achieve some awareness, even if faint, of the existence of our souls. This awareness usually arrives through the simple recognition that beyond the Self, there is something deep within us that we cannot name. For most people who experience them, epiphanies of the soul appear intermittently – whether for a short time or a longer period – and then vanish. These spontaneous bursts of light that some experience cause a sense of spiritual elevation. They do not always involve a feeling of happiness, but they always involve a clarity of vision. We can compare it to the feeling you might have if you stand for a moment at the summit of a mountain, momentarily seeing, breathing, and even feeling differently, perhaps experiencing a sense of liberation.

Another kind of epiphany can be described as just a stirring experience that fills us with a sense of enlightenment and happiness. Or, an epiphany may have a more extreme effect in which the soul's inner light illuminates not only the mind and heart, but produces a heightened sense of experience and consciousness. These epiphanies do not usually occur as the result of a certain action or a specific type of meditation. We experience them as completely spontaneous phenomena that appear, linger for a while, and then fade as suddenly as they appeared.

On the other hand, there are people, probably a minority, to whom the soul reveals itself frequently, consistently, and recognizably. The epiphany of the soul for such individuals is almost like a heartbeat. It accompanies them daily and through every situation, and it has a certain basic permanency. In this type of epiphany, there are normally no exceptional climactic experiences or unusual visions, but simply the general state of being illuminated with inner light, which even others may notice.

In addition to this range of ephemeral epiphanies, it is possible that on any ordinary day – or in the face of a significant, even tragic, incident – you may experience an epiphany and, through it, discover your soul. This would be a dramatic, possibly even terrifying event with no explanation, rational or otherwise, for what occurred – just the feeling that your soul is within you. Through such experiences, which can happen to anyone, you do not discover great mysteries or sudden revelations. Rather, the familiar is suddenly seen in a new light, through different eyes.

An epiphany of the soul can be terrifying because it brings about a new and different perspective on all of reality, on all of life, and it gives rise to the question "What do I do now?" or, "What have I been doing for the last twenty years?" This is reminiscent of the question God asked Adam after the sin in the Garden of Eden: "Where are you?" (Genesis 3:9).

When you hear this voice speaking to you, you may arrive at a disheartening conclusion about the value of your life. The activity of your soul should cause you to rise upward, sensing sanctity, engaging in pursuits whose value is measured in terms other than money and prestige. An epiphany can lead you to ask yourself not only whether you are a sinner or a righteous person, whether you fulfilled your duty or not, but simply, to echo God's call to Adam, "Where are you?" This pithy and elusive question is really asking whether we have achieved what we could have achieved, spiritually, in our lives.

The precise nature of the impact an epiphany may have on you depends on the awareness it brings about in your life. At times, one flash may be enough to shock you into an immediate response. This can feel like walking in the dark when a sudden flash of lightning reveals that you are standing at the edge of an abyss. In this kind of situation, a deep and sustained epiphany is unnecessary. You now realize where you stand, and that is sufficient motivation to pull yourself away from there. For instance, there could be an issue in your life that was never of interest, but now, suddenly, it can no longer be ignored: you are at the edge of an abyss, at the point of no return. The epiphany doesn't reveal anything new; instead, it provides the discovery of an entirely different way of thinking, a realm of the soul that is located on the other side of reality.

This shift can also occur in a different way: instead of the edge of an abyss, you could be making your way through heavy fog. You can discern only blurred figures and images, when suddenly a light appears in the depths of the fog. The light does not change reality but merely provides a new dimension to everything. Objects that had seemed whole now look like parts of larger structures; what had been perceived as walls and partitions now look like entrances and corridors leading to other places. The opposite can also be true: something that used to seem clear and alluring suddenly looks less clear. You might discover, for example, that the path you thought was the only one is really but one of several possible paths, and what had seemed like the highway is actually only a side street.

Such epiphanies, which are actually not so rare, are not necessarily connected with any sort of divine guidance. Rather, they simply offer an entirely different perspective on your whole life.

They may continue to provide significant memories throughout life and enable you to reach for a higher spiritual experience, which serves continuously as a point of comparison.

For many, these epiphanies of the soul are like glimmers of light. They may appear at frequent intervals, or even daily, but they do not always have the power to constitute an ongoing continuousness, or a redemptive experience. They merely accompany us as tiny points of recognition that reality is not limited to the familiar. This is referred to as "fleeting thoughts of repentance," *hirhurei teshuva*, which in many cases do not lead us to a different path but rather reveal the possibility of living differently.

Whether they occur frequently or rarely, we all attain certain epiphanies in our souls. As their frequency and intensity differ among us, so does their effect. Some of us may be capable of grasping these epiphanies and elevating their entire lives to a new level, and others may arrive at only a hazy recognition that there is another kind of existence that remains largely concealed.

Our Sages, who occupied themselves with these aspects of the soul's life, advise us to create spiritual vessels to contain them. When we think about creating spiritual vessels, we can imagine people lost at sea who are hoping to reach a safe haven but who do not have drinking water. If it begins to rain, the initial reaction of these thirsty people will be to open their mouths, cup their hands together, and drink as much of the rainwater as they can. However, the rain will end sooner or later, and only those who found vessels to contain the life-giving water will be able to continue to use it for the duration of their voyage.

Although such vessels cannot really contain the experience, they nevertheless contribute to spiritual growth in a number of significant ways. Spiritual vessels for containing the light of an epiphany could be, for example, a decision to make some change in your way of life, or a far less dramatic decision, say, to begin a certain course of study or to perform certain works. Such a decision – made during one good moment in your life, and causing you to continue acting upon it even after that experience has faded – remains significant for the rest of your life; it preserves a part of the original experience, preventing it from completely fading away. In this way, you guide yourself to a different place, a different world.

Death unravels the connection between the soul and the body, but as long as we are alive, our souls never leave us completely. No matter our character, personality, or deeds, it is impossible for us to reach a state of decline or corruption so profound that we would actually lose our soul. This is because the soul is the foundation of our lives in a far deeper sense than is the manifest Self.

The highly complex structure of body-soul-Self is a synchronized system, and when a certain component upsets the equilibrium, it creates turbulence in the entire system. The classic example of this disruption of equilibrium is prophecy. Testimonies from the period when prophecy occurred demonstrate that neither the soul nor the body was able to contain the prophetic revelation. The Bible describes the prophets falling down or completely losing touch with the outside world. The verse "The prophet is a fool; the man of spirit is mad" (Hosea 9:7) reflects the fact that even if a prophet is a levelheaded, socially involved person – in all other respects a person whose life is in order – when he is under the influence of a prophetic revelation, he becomes an aberration. Prophecy also agitates the nefesh, since it has been inundated with more than it is accustomed to containing, causing the prophet to exhibit signs of madness.

These phenomena, so prominent among prophets, can also manifest themselves in others, at times even in ordinary people who experience some kind of epiphany, whether as the result of a conscious, consistent search or as a flash of light from above. When there is a correlation between the epiphany and the basic spiritual personality of the recipient, that is, the recipient is already given to spiritual reflection, then the experience is positive, but when there is no such correlation, the experience is traumatic for the soul, and perhaps for the body as well. The trauma can create a temporary or permanent fracture in a person's life. Such a fracture is not a punishment. It is, instead, a matter of receiving a gift that is beyond the person's capacity to contain. This can be compared to winning the jackpot in a large lottery. At times, it solves the winner's problems, providing a different life path, but in other cases, particularly because it is not the result of a specific, defined, extended effort, it can cause an existential crisis. Consequently, when our souls are revealed to us through an epiphany, we should pray for the strength to contain it. Even when we ask for something, we must be ready to accept it.

Part II

The Soul and Us

As long as we are alive, our soul is within us at all times, but our attitude toward the soul varies, depending on who we are and the times in which we live. When we are busy with our routine of work, studies, or domestic life, even tangible phenomena such as our breathing and our heartbeat are not always part of our conscious awareness. This is all the more true for the soul, which is largely intangible and toward which we have a complex and equivocal attitude. What's more, it dwells in the hard-to-reach margins of our consciousness, unless remarkable events bring it to the fore.

Our way of life, as well as our specific life paths, all influence our attitude toward the soul. For example, someone who lived one thousand years ago encountered incomparably fewer events, changes, and stimuli than almost every person experiences today. All of this takes both time and attention and does not leave room for many internally focused thoughts. Consequently, while our external reality grows more extensive, more fast-paced, and more demanding, our internal reality is constantly shrinking.

Moreover, a certain aspect of modern life is intentionally structured in a way that prevents people from facing themselves. While people may have more free time, there is a vast and successful industry whose purpose is actually to devour free time. The recreation and entertainment industries are all meant to achieve that goal: to leave us not a tiny space free of pressure, tension, or temptation. These tensions surface in the form of worries and concerns, unpleasant experiences and desires.

Many of the stresses coming at us from every direction are spiritual, so the greatest desire of many of us is to find inner peace. In the past, when the events in people's lives were far more limited, they might have longed for excitement and emotional experiences, but today longings tend to run in the opposite direction: more peace of mind and less stress. It is not surprising that so many pursue pastimes whose main purpose is to calm them down.

Even in days of old, the psalmist prayed, "Return, my soul, to restfulness" (Psalms 116:7). But the soul itself never rests. It is constantly creating and responding both to action and to inaction. And the soul always follows its own course, even when it is not manifest consciously in our thoughts or emotions. Even when we are unaware of what is happening in our soul, the soul tries to make its wishes known and to respond, on its own terms, to what we are doing and feeling. No matter what lifestyle, activities, or conscious thoughts we may have, and no matter what their source, at times the soul within us tries to get our attention and to respond to what is happening in our day-to-day experiences by shouting, "No, no!" or "Yes, this is what you should be doing."

Often the visible reality conceals these utterances of the soul, but they are never completely silenced. Sometimes the soul's messages accumulate within us, not only creating reversals in our thinking but even taking on tangible expression in our lives.

Perfectly clear and fully formed epiphanies of the soul are a vanishingly rare event in general, but they occur fairly frequently in many people in a variety of partial forms. At times, an epiphany will cause us to reject a certain way of life or veer away from it. Other epiphanies may manifest as strong critiques of our life, and at other times an epiphany may present itself in the form of a question: Are the things that occupy me really worth the effort I am investing in them?

These thoughts, which our Sages refer to as *hirhurei teshuva*, fleeting thoughts of repentance, can show up every day, and they may cause great upheaval in our professional or personal lives. Perhaps someone who was a stockbroker decides to leave her job and family and become a painter because her soul won't allow her to remain in a certain area of life while she aspires to a more spiritual existence.

Since these epiphanies are not always sufficiently clear in our conscious understanding, even when they do cause us to make practical and conceptual changes, the changes may manifest themselves as half-baked ideas. The same unconscious messages of the soul can sometimes trigger fears that have no visible cause, but they shake us to the core – even lead to despondency and depression.

Frequently, depression, which is common these days, as evidenced by the huge number of people taking antidepressants or seeking psychiatric treatment, is not necessarily the result of a miserable existence. Instead, it can be part of a relatively peaceful existence in which the soul is trying to say something but isn't getting through. It is rare to find people who exemplify the statement "A person's soul will teach him,"[1] people whose souls guide them toward a certain path or grant them certain insights. In order that "a person's soul will teach him," we must have an open, conscious

---

1. This saying is attributed to the Ba'al Shem Tov, the founder of Hasidism.

dialogue with our soul. When such a dialogue is absent, we are left with fragments that do not provide solutions but raise questions.

The fact that our souls feel a little opaque to us should come as no surprise, since the same situation can exist even with completely material matters. We are aware of most of our visible body parts, but are far less aware of our kidneys and livers and other organs that are hidden inside our bodies. We often become aware of the soul in the same way we become aware of our body's inner organs: when we suffer illness or experience pain in one of them. Indeed, there is no straightforward way that the search for and contemplation of our soul becomes apparent on a conscious level.

When carrying out the search for our souls, we need to be conscious that our dreams and aspirations, even though these are essentially non-material, do not necessarily have anything to do with the soul. Family, education, and various cultural resources, such as books, theater, and so on, are also at work within us and may appear in our thoughts. Therefore, the emergence of new dreams or a longing for something new may not necessarily be spiritual in origin. While it is possible to search within ourselves and find things that are not part of our ordinary reality, many of these are mere reflections of external reality or illusions that lodge themselves within us and are not part of the soul in any fundamental way.

It is possible, therefore, that one who modifies his way of life in some manner as a result of such input is merely realizing an extraneous dream, formed from thoughts and images that came to him from the outside and not from the soul. Indeed, people frequently go off on an adventure in a distant place or break up their families, while in reality they are pursuing an illusion. Even in cases in which the matters at stake are real, these modifications are not always appropriate for the particular individual who is pursuing them. Therefore, even when we isolate ourselves or try to search within ourselves, we should take care not to confuse true, authentic reality with something that was transplanted from outside sources. Often, the soul, or the message it relays, reaches us not as an epiphany but as a disturbance. Our inner reality is exposed when normal, natural consciousness is disrupted or deviates from its path, perhaps for no obvious reason. For instance, a new planet can be discovered as the result of a deviation in the orbit of another, known planet. Likewise, the unusual and the incomprehensible within may lead us to search more carefully for something that exists but is concealed. Every fluctuation in our lives calls upon us to search for its source, sometimes enabling us to discover that what had been bothering us were not emotional problems but various aspirations that were transplanted within us from elsewhere.

As we have seen, it is not easy to discover the soul within us because of the various kinds of background noise that conceal it from us. Only after these noises from the past or present are set aside can we reach a point where we will be able to withstand the ultimate test – the test of truth.

The Soul and God

I F YOUR UNIQUE personality compels you to contemplate your soul in a serious manner, you are probably someone who has a high level of spiritual curiosity, and it is likely that you will reach out to God often – even on an ordinary day. Others, however, need a powerful awakening, a jolting experience of some sort, such as a tragedy or a miracle, to arouse such thoughts.

Such a dramatic experience, no matter when it happens or under what circumstances, will direct our attention to a fundamental focal point that had previously existed only in the back of our minds, if at all. But this is just the beginning of the process. The longer the process lasts, the more it gives rise to new insights and feelings. If, in the past, we might have said, "This topic isn't for me," now a new emotional state dawns. Not only do we begin to understand things in an abstract sense, but we also start to relate to them in a personal, internally focused way. For example, whether we are believers or non-believers, we may have related to the idea that God is the Creator of the universe with the same lack of interest we would show to any mundane facet of life. Suddenly, we move from a state of passive awareness to active contemplation. And we begin to ask questions such as "What does this mean to me?" "What conclusions does this lead me to?" "How does this piece of information change my worldview?"

While passive belief does not create understanding, and certainly not identification, active contemplation inevitably creates something in the soul.

The yearning for God is a feeling that we are not always aware of. At times, we may lack any of the vocabulary or conceptual tools that would be useful in this search; many years may pass until the predisposition of our soul to reach out to God starts to take shape. Moreover, since the soul's tendency is revealed to the Self through our manifest consciousness, the soul's search may go by way of areas that are distant from, and possibly even opposed to, holiness. Furthermore, the act of thinking in itself, no matter how much interest it inspires in us, may lead to different, possibly contradictory conclusions. In this vein, an agnostic, who for some reason doubts God's existence, may become either a believer or an atheist, since atheism, when it is clear and strong, is an expression of the soul's focus on this issue. But in any case, though it may not be completely positive, the transition from agnosticism to atheism shifts the issue from a place of apathy to a place of emotional involvement. Indeed, even the shift from the stage of "What do I care?" to "That angers me" should, in fact, be seen as progress. When we begin to show interest in God and think about Him from time to time, even if it is in an extremely abstract way, we embark on a path that may lead to connecting with God.

Connecting is, in essence, building a relationship. In the traditional liturgy this is referred to as "I and He," *ani vaHu.*[1] The

---

1. This phrase appears in the prayers for the intermediate days of Sukkot, in the *Hoshanot* ritual.

more this relationship is fortified, the less distant and disconnected it becomes. This process strengthens the ties between the Self and the Creator. This kind of connection does not always come about through thinking about it more. It is the result of the essential connection between God and the soul. Since this connection exists in the depths of the nefesh and is not always present in the more accessible levels of consciousness, it needs to be uncovered in order to be awakened. For this purpose, the nefesh is significant because of its close and immediate connection with the Self, which enables it to work directly and not through intermediaries.

All of this relates to the level of the nefesh in itself, independent of the various intellectual and emotional tools that are at its disposal. An intellectual, thinking individual with an undeveloped soul will not reach an intimate connection with God even if he intensifies his efforts and his contemplation. On the other hand, a simple person whose thinking skills and expressive abilities are poor but who possesses a sensitive soul can achieve a great awakening.

Just as these matters are unrelated to the various tools available to the nefesh, so are they unrelated to age, maturity, and experience. A small child whose thinking skills have not reached maturity may achieve a higher spiritual level than those who are older and wiser. However, one who both possesses the proper tools and also makes use of them can undoubtedly reach a higher level of understanding and a greater intensity of experience than a naturally spiritual, but not contemplative, person.

This deliberate effort to progress spiritually may be compared to the actualization of various abilities that lie dormant within almost every individual. We all have numerous capabilities that are part of our genetic makeup but which do not spontaneously reveal themselves. Some need cultivation and education to be actualized. Similarly, the capacities of the soul may not become apparent to us unless they have been cultivated and cared for.

Ideally, we are aware of our soul's power in all of its intensity, and as a result, our entire personality turns toward it. However, even at this ideal level, the soul does not intrude upon the Self or attempt to change its course. Even someone whose soul reveals itself so clearly may not be well suited for the clergy, for example. The choice of such a lifestyle depends not only on the soul itself but on many worldly factors that don't necessarily involve sanctity. In some places, for instance, religious roles have social significance requiring certain intellectual and social skills, and many a holy soul would be unqualified to fill such religious positions.

Similarly, not in every society can an individual be exclusively involved in matters of sanctity. It depends on whether that society will support and assist him. So even when someone's soul is impelled toward sanctity, it does not necessarily determine that person's profession or personality. Such a person, in fact, could spend a lifetime in pursuits that may be perfectly honorable but unrelated to sanctity, say, as a teacher or counselor, a farmer or factory worker, a community or political leader.

The difference between someone who is driven by his soul and others in the same profession has nothing to do with the quality or trajectory of their work; rather, it has to do with intent. An example of this can be found in the Midrash about Enoch, an ancestor of Noah. The Sages say that he turned into an angel, but during his lifetime in this world, he worked as a shoemaker.[2] The opposite is true as well. There are people who have religiously ori-

---

2. Genesis 5:21–24 and R. Menaḥem da Fano, *Ma'amar Em Kol Ḥai* 3:22; *Zohar*, Genesis 27:1; see the commentary of *Recanati* on Genesis 5:22.

ented professions even though their souls illuminate them only a little and they do not have a deep connection with what they are doing, even when they do it well. As to character, a person with a holy soul doesn't have to be taciturn and introspective. Nothing in a holy soul precludes dedication to family and friends; such a soul may even have a sense of humor.

Every one of us, whoever and wherever we may be, lives in a material world that requires specific conduct. When we stand or sit, eat or sleep, we do so in accordance with the rules governing the world we happen to live in. But the fact that we live by the rules of our material existence does not mean we spend time thinking about it. The totality of the world simply exists, and those living within it are not necessarily distinctly aware of it. The same is true of the social structures within which we live. The existence of these structures creates countless, detailed rules of conduct. But we who live within society are not necessarily conscious of society in general, even our own.

When we lead a good and honest life, whether we were born into it and raised within it or whether we reached it on our own, the focus of our search for God is sharpened. For people educated in a world of faith in which there is more room for God, this is more natural and obvious. But living in an environment of faith does not necessarily improve our odds of reaching our spiritual goals. In fact, what is often referred to as "religious society" is not necessarily a place where much attention is paid to spirituality. The frequent observance of commandments of all types, within any faith or belief, does create religious frameworks, habits, and modes of expression, but does not necessarily lead to actual holiness as expressed in an individual person.

It might be surprising to learn that you can observe numerous commandments and pray frequently but still be unaware of what you are saying and doing. You can live your entire life in a completely religious world without ever thinking about the essence of this world or its underlying meaning. Such a way of life is similar to our relationship to the sun. The sun illuminates everything, and at times we may mention its brightness or heat, but we do not necessarily devote time or effort to thinking about it. It exists, it functions, and that's it.

Our attitude toward religion and belief in God is largely dependent on culture and education, and on the period in which we live. In some eras of history, belief in God was prevalent, perhaps almost universal, while in other eras, the opposite was the case. We are not talking about faith in its general sense here, since the human capability and desire to believe seems to have existed throughout history and to encompass all ideologies. The prevalence of superstitions and adherence to them has not changed much in the last five thousand years. What do change are the forms assumed by these beliefs. Whether they exist or not, demons always continue to be active; they merely appear with different masks and disguises in each generation. The idea that one day people will be free of all types of belief and will deal with life's issues in an exclusively rational manner seems as impossible today as it did in the past. On the contrary, this aspiration itself is but one of the plethora of beliefs in the world.

Or we might reframe the subject of our discussion in this chapter as the relationship between our soul and our perception of the Divine. We could say, for instance, that everything we have discussed so far relates to the place of faith in the life of the nefesh, of which we are often conscious. It is, however, unrelated to any discussion of the influence of faith on the soul. Its full power may often be obscured from view, but the influence of the soul is still felt, both within the depths of the nefesh and also in plain view within reality. The soul, impelled to reach upward (see Ecclesiastes 3:21), has a certain contact with a deeper reality, or at the very least, an inner drive and a longing for the ultimate reality, however we might understand it. Therefore, even when our education or society diverts attention from our soul, a conscious recognition of God can still be discovered in various situations.

Such discoveries do not normally occur as the result of searching for a solution to concrete problems, but mostly in situations of distress, illness, or uncertainty about our goals in life. In such instances, something within the nefesh is somehow thrown into relief, or becomes more poignant, even when our philosophical background, or even just sheer existence, obscures it. As the saying goes, there are no atheists in foxholes. But to a certain extent, even though it is not as common, such a sensation can also arise in times of tranquility, relief, and even great happiness.

In a sense, an epiphany of the soul is like a reaction to a life-threatening situation. Our objective defects and blemishes are temporarily forgotten, and even people who suffer from pain or disabilities find themselves running or jumping, completely forgetting the pain and limitations of the body. The description of the prophet Isaiah "Then the lame will leap like a deer" (Isaiah 35:6) describes not only a miracle experienced by the lame person, but also a tremendous emotional awakening in which this person, whether physically or spiritually lame, somehow transcends this facet of existence. On the physiological level, a huge amount of adrenaline courses through the body, while in the soul, an epiphany takes place, affecting the person's spiritual perception.

Such an epiphany does not always merely involve a new perspective. It could be a manifestation of something from deep within us that we may not be familiar with. Since this inner energy operates with hardly any connection to our conscious perception, these episodes may happen in people who do not even define themselves as believers or as religious. There were thousands, perhaps hundreds of thousands, of Jews across many generations who sacrificed their lives for the sanctification of God's name, and only a fraction of them had lived lives of holiness. On the contrary, it appears that even those who had never shown any propensity for matters of faith or holiness may have discovered in themselves something greater and more exalted than they could fully grasp: the need to sacrifice everything, including their lives, for the sanctification of God's name. These incidents do not involve great conscious clarity or a specific vision, but an epiphany whose relationship with the ethereal spheres is not always clear or rational. And these epiphanies are sufficient to enable a person to determine what direction to take in extreme circumstances.

Examples of this phenomenon can be found throughout the history of the Jewish people from Yosef MeShita, who was murdered by the Roman destroyers of the Temple for refusing to reenter the Temple sanctuary to plunder its holy objects,[3] to Daniel Pearl, an assimilated Jewish journalist who was kidnapped and murdered in Pakistan in 2002, whose last words were "My name is Daniel Pearl. I am an American Jew. My father is Jewish, my mother's Jewish, I'm Jewish."

The soul's relationship to the Ultimate Source is part of its very being, but the degree to which this relationship is revealed to us depends on the degree to which the soul, itself, is accessible to us. As we have seen, in an environment where there is no place for a spiritual world, or in a society in which all the accepted values are material and utilitarian, there is much less room for the soul to manifest itself.

---

3. See *Genesis Rabba* 65:22.

The Soul and Its Garments

T HE ESSENCE OF the soul is distinct from the collection of attributes that we might call its "garments." The garments of the soul are characteristics and abilities belonging to a certain soul, the Self properties of a particular soul within a particular body. These can include various behaviors and personality traits; they can include awareness, emotions, and memory; and they can also include speech and action.

Garments of the soul are material or semi-material, and therefore, like the body, they are subject to the laws of biology and genetics: just as people inherit their eye color, height, and facial features from their parents, so do they inherit from them the capabilities whose origins are genetic. Although we have no clear data regarding the heredity of spiritual capabilities, the garments of the soul are influenced not only by genetic properties but also by upbringing and education. Because of this, children with fairly similar spiritual capabilities can develop in completely different ways depending on the educational and family environments in which they are raised. A child with average talents who is raised in a family that hones these talents will usually develop more fully than a talented child who grows up in a family that lacks the social or economic means to help develop those skills. Another variable factor in the garments of the soul is related to behaviors and character traits, such as diligence, persistence, and laziness, which also depend on genetics, environment, and education.

It is possible to understand the concept of garments of the soul when we become familiar with the factors giving rise to them, but from the point of view of the soul's essence, garments do not belong to the soul itself. Consequently, extrinsic factors have only a limited influence on the soul. Thus, we may follow a virtuous path, even the path of Torah and observance of the commandments. As far as the soul's garments (e.g., education and development) are concerned, we might achieve, through this path, the maximum our extrinsic talents allow, but we cannot change the essence of our soul.

The actual attributes of the soul, which are not the same as its garments, create part of our emotional and intellectual makeup. Certain souls originate in the characteristic of loving-kindness, or *ḥesed*. Therefore, they will express this characteristic throughout their lives, both in their conduct and in their way of understanding things around them. Others, who are chiefly rooted in the characteristic of fortitude, or *gevura*, will express that trait in their deeds and worldview. The same applies to all people, whether their souls originate in the characteristic of generosity or frugality, leniency or severity, and so on. Each of these characteristics is morally neutral; each expresses a fundamental way of being that can manifest itself in a positive or in a negative way.

People notice different aspects of reality in accordance with the foundational aspect of their souls. We also orient our speech and actions around these aspects, even building our worldview upon them. Here, too, when the basic components of the soul are amplified by genetics and environment, they manifest themselves more clearly, whereas within those whose inner existence and garments of the soul are in conflict, these attributes will be more subdued.

The relationship between the soul and its external garments may create a life narrative that is marked by asymmetry. A person with a soul that is intensely drawn to holiness but who is born into a family with no relationship to sanctity may spend years, even an entire lifetime, attempting to resolve the inner contradiction between the orbit of the soul and its extrinsic garments. Exceptionally lofty souls may be born in a place that not only fails to cultivate such garments, but actually causes them to degenerate.

When it is dressed in the appropriate garments, the soul's greatness may be revealed at a very tender age. Indeed, there are many people whose talents and spiritual depth were apparent even in their early years. However, when such a soul appears in a place where it lacks the appropriate social, educational, or cultural background, it is forced to fight within the extrinsic structures that limit it and throttle its capabilities. Thus the constant tension between the soul's lofty essence on the one hand, and its garments and limited means of expression on the other, may delay its manifestation.

This can be likened to a person with exceptional artistic talent who lacks the tools and materials to express her art. She will need to struggle within the limitations of the tools and materials at her disposal to create what she is truly capable of, and even then her essence may remain unarticulated. Conversely, others who are not endowed with exceptional talent may have achieved much, taking an active role in the world and influencing others, and expressing their soul's essential nature to a greater degree.

A similar distinction exists between what we could call holy souls and souls that are not oriented toward holiness, that is, between souls that, beyond the existence of the soul itself, do (or do not) possess a special sensitivity to the sacred. The holy soul, especially that of a righteous person, can be likened to the essence of a musical genius, whose unique quality is not necessarily an inborn talent but an unusual sensitivity to music itself and a great desire for it. We could think of a person with a holy soul as a genius for holiness. Even in the absence of education, environment, or genetics, such a person is attracted to holiness and is able to appreciate holy things.

When such a soul is manifest, it becomes meaningful, both for itself and for others. But since this manifestation relates to the soul and not necessarily to its garments, a person with a holy soul may not be aware of its unique essence and may not necessarily have access to the tools or environments that would provide the structure and clarity to perceive it. Those of us who have a high or a holy soul may live with a sense that there is something inside that cannot be expressed, an unidentified desire, a vague awareness that we are different from others. We may experience a complex, tumultuous life in which we always sense that we are on the wrong path.

Indeed, part of our inner work in this world is adapting the various garments to the essence of our soul, since the soul itself is always greater, holier, and more stable than any of the garments it acquires along the way.

The Soul and Character Traits

THE MOST COMMON outward manifestation of the nefesh within us is our *middot*, or character traits. Compassion, gentleness, sensitivity, cruelty, inflexibility, decisiveness, consideration of others, and other traits are not only the most basic manifestations of our inner reality, but they actually define it. We can therefore say that the "*middot* of the nefesh," as this idea appears in traditional Jewish literature, define the structure of the personality. Essentially, our *middot* do not relate to us; they are the tools through which we relate to reality as a whole, and to other people in particular, whether those others are close or distant, whether they are relatives, friends, or enemies.

While the *middot* that make up the various aspects of our personality are innate and are generated in the core of our soul, the differences between individuals result not only from the singularity of each and every soul but also from factors that are more or less external. For example, as we said in the previous chapter, both genetics and education have a tremendous impact on *middot*, which are also affected by someone's situation in the world in general and within society in particular. Accordingly, just as a society may educate its members to be compassionate and sensitive, it may likewise educate them to be cruel and self-ish. An example of such an all-inclusive educational process is that of ancient Sparta, which included not only specific physical exercises and nutritional habits but also modes of speech and relating to others.

Human genetics are not yet well understood, especially in relation to phenomena that are more complex than, say, eye color or the shape of our noses. Nevertheless, it is generally understood that genetics inform not only our intellectual ability but also our basic emotional makeup. As a result, some cannot express their feelings often, while others express themselves quickly and eas-ily. Certain character traits themselves can be considered heredi-tary: compassion or cruelty, assertiveness or meekness, and so on. Indeed, sometimes entire families possess these or other traits. What's more, heredity determines the tools that the nefesh uses to respond to the stimuli it encounters.

Despite the great impact of education and genetics, how-ever, these influences do not entirely determine the content of *middot*. Beyond the things we inherit in the material and spiritual spheres, we are also influenced by the way we each develop organi-cally throughout our lives. At times, the soul's teachings divert us entirely from the way of life that was laid out by others and lead us instead on a new, unknown path. As is said in the name of the Ba'al Shem Tov, "A person's soul will teach him."[1] Sometimes the soul's teachings appear only sporadically, perhaps causing us to respond differently than we would expect to respond. For example,

---

1. Attributed to the Ba'al Shem Tov in the additions to *Keter Shem Tov* 223.

feelings of compassion or love may begin to flow within the hearts of people unaccustomed to these feelings, perhaps even leading them to change their lives.

The soul is not a set of responses to external stimuli. It has its own essence and characteristics that function beyond traits that are passed down genetically or taught. So "a person's soul will teach him" applies even when the soul does not speak clearly or explicitly. The soul's direction is essentially upward, yet hidden in its depths there are guiding elements about what is appropriate for us to do in the physical world. In other words, we could say that our souls teach us about the existence of the heavenly realm and simultaneously about the existence of other people. Therefore, despite the fact that people are born with the trait of selfishness, or exhibit it later in life, the soul opens the mind's eye so that we do not merely notice others but are also able to understand and empathize with them. Accordingly, although there are parts within us that are based solely on calculations of narrow benefit, the soul also conveys to us messages concerning absolute values. When we are unaware of our soul, we lead lives that revolve around self-fulfillment; we may even think of our lives solely in monetary terms. But there is also an inner reality, and it is that reality that defines a human as such and arouses within us the awareness of what the soul aspires to.

What are referred to as good *middot*, that is, a refined character, depend largely on the soul's influence. If we have bad *middot*, and negative character traits seem natural and acceptable to us, then we are probably oblivious to our soul. We can defend this ourselves by saying, "This is my nature," or, "That is how I was raised," but these are merely excuses. The wisest of men, King Solomon, said, "A fool has no delight in understanding, but only that his heart may lay itself bare" (Proverbs 18:2). It is certainly possible to function on the level of "laying his heart bare," both intellectually and emotionally. But we must conclude that, even if our hearts tell us in the most straightforward manner to behave in a certain way, it may be that what is leading us to that behavior are acquired characteristics that are not authentic elements expressing the essence of our soul, but in fact superficial structures contrived for our own benefit, to protect our status or to bolster us in our struggle for survival. In any case, when we become aware of certain unsavory *middot* in our own character, we should know that these are not superficial behaviors or habits, but indications of a deficiency in our soul's manifestation.

The search for our soul is not necessarily meant to express itself in a quest for spiritual or religious experiences. Our soul, to the extent that it is active within us, does push us toward spiritual elevation, however, and also changes our essence in the present. In addition to detailed commandments, the Torah includes general ones such as "And you shall do what is right and good" (Deuteronomy 6:18). Underlying these general commandments is the assumption that we are capable of reaching the "right and good" by means of our own soul.

It follows that if we are aware of our soul, we are required to examine the parts within ourselves that are lacking in goodness and righteousness. And it behooves us to do this because these imperfections are signs that the soul has failed to manifest itself. If we are stingy because of education or heredity, for instance, we can become aware of the recognition that this trait is not the way of the soul. If we are cruel, we can be aware that this characteristic does not originate in the soul but is rather a personality defect that we can correct. And if we are deceitful, we can understand that this behavior is not merely the result of some technical failure to comply with a clause in a book of laws, but stems from the inability of the soul to recognize the honesty of the heart. And we can correct this, too.

It appears, then, that our *middot* are the place where we confront our soul. *Middot* determine what a person is, far more than abstract contemplation or intellectual evaluations. Unfortunately, for many people the soul rarely glimmers. Our work in this world – with our souls and with our *middot* – has the potential to change that. Do we want to remain in a state of animalistic non-reflectiveness, or do we want to become someone in whom the soul glimmers?

Souls and Their Roots

ALTHOUGH OUR SOULS are always guiding us somehow, actually understanding this guidance is another matter. In generations past, people would make an enormous effort to travel to a great Hasidic Rebbe, not in order to ask him what to do in a particular situation, and not even to receive guidance. Their purpose was to become more familiar with the essence of their own souls by being in the presence of such a lofty personality.

The characteristics of the soul itself are abstract and, therefore, subject to interpretation. And, since most souls are combinations of various spiritual elements, it is not always easy for us to recognize our soul's major components. But when we succeed in understanding something of our soul's essence, this consciousness can guide us as we make our way through the vicissitudes of our lives. In the physical world, it is useful to have a basic map that outlines the directions in which we wish to travel. Likewise, in our inner lives, it is worthwhile to have a map, of sorts, that outlines the spiritual paths that our souls deem best for us. Without such a map, it often happens that our soul intends for us to develop a certain kind of emotional life, but we end up taking a completely different path because of the kind of education we received or any number of other reasons.

For example, perhaps you belong to the world of prayer, according to the root of your soul, but maybe you were raised in a world that led you in a literary direction instead, or your own talents may have led you in such a direction. So, even if you distinguish yourself in the world of literature, your achievements are not necessarily related to the root of your soul. While you are capable of succeeding in these literary pursuits, they are not what your soul requires of you. For this reason, our spiritual quests have practical ramifications. They determine what we should be doing according to the roots of our souls, and they are especially significant when we have no external guidance to lead us on an authentic path.

This kind of predicament is illustrated in a story about a follower of Rabbi Yehuda Aryeh Leib Alter, the author of the *Sefat Emet*. In his younger years, this man reached great heights in his Torah studies. One day, he was asked to be the rabbi of a community. When he went to Rabbi Yehuda Aryeh Leib to ask for a blessing that he be successful in his new position, his Rebbe, surprisingly, told him that according to the root of his soul, he should become a shoemaker. Although the young man possessed all the skills necessary to be a rabbi, the Rebbe saw that his soul required that he be involved not in the rabbinate but rather in productive labor. Consequently, the young man declined the rabbinic appointment, learned the art of shoemaking, and was thus occupied for the rest of his life. What's more, each year he would present the Rebbe with a new pair of shoes.

When we are faced with such an impossible situation and feel incapable of making a rational decision, we should decide what to do according to the basic inclination of our soul, from whose perspective matters are self-evident. Of course, gaining access to that perspective is not necessarily easy, as we have seen. In the literature of the Kabbalah,[1] precise divisions relating to the root of the soul are sketched out. In these works, we see some souls that are of the essence of the biblical Cain's soul and other souls that are of the essence of his brother Abel's soul. These two soul types exist at all times, and both turn heavenward, but their paths and characters differ. Souls of Cain's essence are by nature fiercer and perhaps more creative than souls of Abel's essence, and everything they do will manifest this inner aspect of theirs, while the souls of Abel's essence are more tender and more fully formed, revealing themselves in a way that is in keeping with their source.

When we are aware of our own essence, we can try to build an outer and inner life accordingly, so that we indeed follow the path that is suitable for the roots of our souls.

DIFFERING SOULS

The way each soul manifests itself is unique. Much has been written about the differing sources from which souls originate. There is a kabbalistic notion that the source of souls is in the combinations, or *yiḥudim*, of the *sefirot*, or divine emanations. Souls are not identical to the *sefirot*, but they are derived from them. In other words, souls originate in the garments of the *sefirot*.[2] Every *sefira* has an essential definition that, to a certain extent, is its garment, that is to say, its way of revealing itself in the world. These garments are the source from which souls are brought forth. At times, a soul emanates from a single *sefira*; consequently, there is a single, specific source of its yearnings and impulses. But most souls are made up of combinations of a number of *sefirot* that compose their inner essence. The souls of some, for example, originate in the aspect of

---

1. See, for example, *Sha'ar HaGilgulim*, by Rabbi Ḥayyim Vital. – Ed.
2. *Etz Ḥayyim, Sha'ar HaIbburim*, chap. 1 and passim.

loving-kindness, ḥesed, so that they will manifest themselves, both emotionally and consciously, through a tendency toward loving-kindness. Other souls originate in the aspect of strength, *gevura*, so that they will be manifest, whether in personal experience or spiritual awareness, through the medium of strength. In fact, it is said that the difference between the house of Shammai and the house of Hillel had nothing to do with differing levels of greatness or holiness, but was related, instead, to the roots of their souls, which led them to act and think in a certain way.[3]

Every soul has a definition, whether it is simple or more complex, and every soul reveals the traits of its fundamental *sefirot* by means of its unique selfhood. Therefore, even when there are several people whose existence is largely shaped by, say, the *sefira* of loving-kindness, or ḥesed, they will still be different from one another. Even a single spiritual trait can have an endless number of expressions because our minds and our free will, as well as heredity and education, can cause that trait to incline in different directions. For example, a soul whose essence is ḥesed might express itself through acts of kindness for everyone, or by wasting energy and resources on unimportant matters. The fundamental trait may be the same, but it will appear in different forms and qualities.

The knowledge that souls are different from one another doesn't always come from the outside; at times this knowledge may come from familiarity with ourselves. You may have the gift of an extremely developed nefesh, through which you achieve genuine greatness in many areas, yet you yourself may be aware that the soul part within you is not particularly manifest. It is equally possible that you did not receive such gifts in either body or nefesh, but nevertheless you are imbued with a lofty soul, even though you may not be aware of it. The thirty-six hidden *tzaddikim*, or

---

3. *Ben Porat Yosef, Parashat Mikketz.*

righteous people, upon whom the entire world depends[4] are often themselves unaware of who they are, since the manifestation of the soul also requires the appropriate emotional background and active awareness, which may be lacking.

As we have said, our souls involve diverse elements. Nevertheless, each of us perceives our own soul, with all its complexity and intricacies, as one single presence. Only as we grow and mature, however, can we perceive the souls of others, and most of the time, we do not feel the soul of another person directly. We just assume that it exists within the other, just as it exists within ourselves. But every human interaction, even though it is not a direct meeting of one soul with another, involves a manifestation of the souls of two people. When we smile or frown at each other, we are trying to transmit some kind of message to one another. In a deeper sense, we are trying to transmit a message from one soul to another. When we speak, we are certainly trying to communicate to others some information that is hidden within our own souls.

Children, or even adults who have not yet lost their naïveté, may feel that they are indeed able to create a soul-to-soul dialogue. At any age, we might feel that a direct soul-to-soul communication has taken place through bonds of friendship, of connected thinking, of unified action, or of love. But with time and experience, especially when we begin to think deeply about this issue, we discover that we are not involved in soul-to-soul contact at all. The soul has many garments of its own, but it continues to acquire more and more of them with time and experience. This is why most human contact, even with those who are closest to us, is at best a kind of embrace between two people, both of whom are dressed in several layers of clothing.

---

4. Based on Talmud *Sanhedrin* 97b.

However, this does not mean that you can't build a soul bond with another person. On the contrary, deep and meaningful relationships can be formed over time. But even when people are willing to bare their souls to one another and share with one another the soul's garments – the garments of awareness, emotions, and memory – they can still feel between their souls that essential distance, a distance that makes direct contact impossible. Not only in normal situations, when souls reveal themselves to one another through their extrinsic garments (that is, through action or speech), but even in those exceptional cases when one soul can sense the thoughts of the other – even then, the information is transmitted between their souls through the intermediary of garments. While these garments constitute a vehicle that enables people to connect with one another, they also create the differences between them. Indeed, even those who are capable of comprehending the thinking of others, because they are blessed with a subtle understanding or a sixth sense, know that this contact is not completely transparent.

SPIRITUAL CLOSENESS

But despite all the uniqueness and differences, there are souls that are similar, or connected, to one another. Souls that stem from the same root or are built from similar components become closer to each other within the reality of this world and share certain tendencies, exhibiting, beyond this basic closeness, a common direction that they choose to take in the world.

As we have seen, people don't usually form truly deep and meaningful, soul-level bonds with each other. We do not usually relate to each other's souls at all. Nevertheless, our relationships with others are not limited to doing business; we also learn from others, and even like them. Indeed, it often happens that people want to be close to each other, whether through a loving relationship or a deep friendship, and they try to find a connection that is

beyond the external, obvious characteristics of the other, a connection that involves the other's soul as well. This opens the possibility of a relationship that is much closer. However, even when
we begin to relate to the manifestations of the nefesh of another
person, this still does not necessarily create contact between souls.
For such contact to occur, both sides must consciously invest in
self-exposure. People can, for example, tell their lawyer about their
crimes against society, or discuss their emotional problems with
their psychologist, but this is just a manifestation of a certain part
of the Self that is defined according to circumstances. Even in an
ordinary relationship, we can be completely familiar with each
other's history or the extent of each other's knowledge – and at
times even their entire repertoire of jokes – but this is still not a
spiritual connection. After all, exposing our souls even to ourselves is not part of the course of normal life, let alone exposing
our souls to someone else.

All of us have aspects of our soul that we do not wish to
reveal – and also lack the ability to reveal. This arises both from
our desire to keep private areas to ourselves and from the fact that
we, ourselves, are only partially familiar with our own soul. We
all have elevated elements and base elements. We are generally
unaware of these, but they may be revealed under particular circumstances.[5] All of this is part of the mystery of human existence,
in which all of these layers are acting within us, even when they
are not revealed outwardly. Due to the limits that are inherent in
interpersonal contact, we each recognize the "otherness" of the
other at some stage, a recognition that no two people are identi-

---

5. This is what the Sages meant in the following passage: "In three matters a person's
true character is ascertained: In his cup (*koso*) [i.e., his behavior when he drinks], in
his pocket (*kiso*) [i.e., his conduct in his financial dealings with other people], and
in his anger (*ka'aso*)" (Talmud *Eiruvin* 65b). This refers to the aspects of the person
that his Self is normally not conscious of.

cal even in the revealed parts of their nefesh, and all the more so in its concealed parts. We understand that there are as many souls in the world as there are human beings and that they differ from one another in as many ways.

But despite the unique quality of each soul, even a casual observer can see that souls can be categorized, with regard to both their level and the basic characteristics that define them.

It could be said that the meeting of souls entails far more intimate contact than any other encounter, physical or spiritual, since it involves revealing the truly concealed part of our existence. At times, though not always, such a coming together can take place between partners in a loving relationship, or within a close friendship where nefesh clings to nefesh, which is what may be meant by the phrase in the verse "your friend that is like your own soul [nefesh]" (Deuteronomy 13:7). At other times, this bond can be formed between students, or Hasidim and their Rebbe. These spiritual encounters, while not very common, are intense, and they create a closeness that cannot be achieved in any other way. But even those whose spiritual characteristics are very similar do not always reach this depth. People often feel a yearning for this kind of connection, but usually it does not happen on its own; it requires conscious effort from both sides, and even when we really want to raise a relationship to such a level, we do not always succeed.

Happy are those who merit experiencing "your friend that is like your own soul," however it may come about!

Selfishness

T HE SOUL POSSESSES virtues and abilities; it also has defects, the most prominent of which is selfishness. Those aspects of behavior and personality that relate to selfishness are usually defects not of the godly soul (neshama) itself but of the vital soul (nefesh). Traits such as arrogance, boastfulness, lack of compassion, and inability to empathize with the suffering of others are certainly related to selfishness. These are not basic traits, however, but far more complex constructs based on other aspects of the nefesh. While they are indeed based on a certain weakness of the soul, they do not belong to the soul's essence.

Selfishness is a distortion of the nefesh. In this state, instead of serving as a meeting point between a human being and God, the nefesh becomes trapped in the lower elements of the Self – the ego – as well as the inherently problematic nature of the body; it becomes lost in physicality, thereby impeding the ability of the soul to express itself. While the nefesh is in some way involved in our illnesses and problems, our spiritual defects arise from the nature of the soul's contact with the nefesh. There are many factors that may divert the soul from its path, but all of these are extrinsic factors that result from the soul's entanglement with the more superficial tendencies of the nefesh.

Selfishness is a spiritual problem because it relates to the way the soul is manifest within us. Before a fetus is born, there is nothing in its world other than itself. That is why a newborn baby comprehends only "me." This has nothing to do with character or even with the soul; it is simply a fact. The fetus's awareness, to the extent that it exists, is very dim. When a newborn baby is exposed to the world in which everything is "the other," all other existences are foreign. It is only through a slow, gradual process that a young child's consciousness acquires the ability to make thoughtful distinctions.

The formation of a child's persona, however, is to a great extent determined by the depth of the child's soul. A child who is spoiled by the entire family will not necessarily grow up to be a selfish child or adult. Conversely, a child who is never coddled and who, from an early age, is taught to share his life and belongings with others will not necessarily grow up to be a more sharing person.

The quality of the soul is, therefore, what determines how we navigate reality. In other words, the answer to the question of whether the personality that emerges will be selfish and self-centered or more open to others probably depends on the nature of the soul. The conditions in which our consciousness and thinking develop will, in turn, intensify the soul's development in a given direction. Indeed, the ego is the focal point of all people, not only in the early stages of development, but often throughout our entire lives, such that the attention of the ego to itself is natural and obvious. But it is not inevitable that every individual will become egocentric. Moreover, even one who tends toward selfishness may change with time. Our thinking and understanding, as well as the work of our soul, have the power to release us from the shackles of selfishness and lead us to a different spiritual arena.

Society, with all its rules and conventions, usually softens and limits the external expressions of egocentrism. Even animals in a herd limit themselves in accordance with the group they belong to. Small children also develop a certain degree of connectedness and a feeling of commonality. Through the ages, different models of human society have emerged. There are societies in which egocentrism is the accepted mode of behavior. This is the case, for example, in societies of warriors or bandits, and even in some aristocracies. In all of these cultures, which operate according to the principle of privilege, selfishness is normal. On the other hand, there are societies that emphasize sensitivity and consideration for others. However, even in a society that emphasizes sharing, there will always be egocentric people. The most talented among them may become leaders, while those with less talent will simply be unpleasant to be around, even if they will not always be able to fulfill all their wishes.

Even the most blatant selfishness, however, is not necessarily the desire to do evil. Even extreme egocentrism is not intended to harm others, since the selfish person acts selfishly solely for narrow benefit.

The problems arising from exclusive focus on one's self cannot be dealt with through psychological analysis alone, because while the soul is clearly connected to the Self (as the symbiosis of body and soul – see the chapter titled "The Manifest Soul"), it must not be mistaken for the Self, per se. If we equate the Self with the manifestation of the soul, we are detracting from the value of the soul and limiting it to a specific, defined area. For the soul is not only our unique essence; it is also the clearest revelation of Godliness in the world. God exists beyond all worlds and yet is within all worlds, as a constant, active force, and He can also be found within the human soul.

Looking to the creation of mankind, the Torah states: "[The Lord God] breathed into his nostrils the breath of life" (Genesis 2:7). The Sages understood this to mean that God figuratively gave part of His living soul to create man's living soul. The soul is unique, for it contains something that does not exist anywhere else except within God Himself: free will. Expressed differently, the godly component in our soul is what gives us the incredible power to create. Other living creatures also possess a certain level of creativity, but only human beings can develop their intellectual and practical abilities to a degree similar to that of the Creator of the universe. And since the soul contains, at least in potential, a kernel of infinity, identifying the soul with anything else, no matter what it may be, detracts from its own character.

Indeed, one of the fundamental problems of morality in general, and of mystical-moral thought in particular, is dealing with the "I-ism," the exclusive focus on the narrow self. This is because when the ego becomes the central force in our lives, our souls become servants of a limited presence. Even if a specific Self is deep and elevated and encompasses a whole world, it will never be as large as infinity. The high regard in which many cultures in the world – and certainly Judaism as well – hold the trait of humility stems from that very same point: humility is not just one good trait among the large array of character traits a person may acquire; it is the essential one. Even Maimonides, an avid supporter of the "golden mean," who calls for restraint and moderation with regard to all character traits and sensibilities, says that humility knows no bounds, and that when it comes to humility, we should not adopt a path of moderation but veer toward the extreme.[1] Indeed, the loftiest figure in our tradition is Moses, and he is praised specifically for his humility. He is the only person of whom it is said:

---

1. Maimonides, *Mishne Torah, Sefer HaMadda, Hilkhot Deot* 2:3.

"The man...was very humble, more than any person on the face of the earth" (Numbers 12:3).

When we achieve a spiritual awakening, we become aware of our ego as a significant obstacle in our ascent. The soul's enslavement to the ego is the most difficult and burdensome thing for it to overcome on its upward journey. Many view the battle against the ego as a war against evil inclinations and material temptations. However, even when we are successful in breaking one evil inclination or another, there still seems to be an impediment within us that is not a specific inclination but simply the ego itself. Indeed, even those of us who are able to expand our nefesh to an exceptional degree by deep thinking or creativity are still unable to free ourselves from this enslavement.

The ego participates in every thought and judgment call, even among completely normal people. Pride is merely an outburst of the ego flowing from our attitude toward it and our overidentification with it. Nevertheless, whether we are great or small, famous or obscure – no matter what path we take in our search for the revelation of the soul – we constantly encounter the stumbling block of the ego.

A significant step on every path to the soul, then, is the intellectual and emotional effort we give to limiting the power of the ego. This enterprise is known as "self-nullification," or *bittul hayesh*, and it is at the core of our spiritual striving. It does not involve minimizing our identity to become nothing; rather, it is a process that is meant to limit the control of the ego. This task of controlling the ego is a universal human task, relevant also to those who do not have a special weakness in this area, but all the more so when the ego exceeds its proper dimensions. When it reaches this point, it becomes not merely an obstacle on the path to spiritual growth but the epitome of spiritual degeneration.

We human beings are full of deficiencies and negative inclinations of all types that can become obstacles for all of us. In our quest for spiritual growth, our attempt to limit the ego is a more important task than anything else. Attempting to conceal selfishness in various ways is no solution; the rectification of this character trait requires a profound, inwardly directed emotional effort. It is said of humanity: "You have made him but a little lower than God" (Psalms 8:6). Perhaps in response to this, there is a temptation, perhaps the most profound and basic temptation of all, to equate ourselves with God.

We are born with the ego and also grow into it. As a result, many other inclinations are awakened within us. The soul's vulnerability is that whenever it is not sufficiently manifest, it becomes enslaved. This is a structural weakness we are required to resist, just as we are meant to struggle within the complex reality of body and soul. Setting limits and boundaries for the ego so that it does not turn our soul into a tool in the service of a foreign god is therefore a fundamental task for us all, and it is a struggle faced exclusively by the human race.

What Afflicts the Soul?

THROUGH OUR DEEDS, we can ignore our souls completely. We can act as we please, occupying ourselves with trivial things (or important things), without the soul revealing its presence within us. In this respect, we can once again compare the function of the soul in our lives to body parts whose existence and functions we are unaware of until an ailment in one of them brings us to death's door.

Every one of us suffers from pain related to the soul in some way or other almost every day of our lives. Severe anguish of the soul can result from personal tragedies, from an inability to withstand life's trials, or from confronting realities that hurt us in some way. These are the pains of the manifest soul, and all this is part of what transpires in the soul at its most basic level, which as you remember from the chapter "What Is the Soul?" is called the vital soul, or nefesh. These pains are unrelated to the deeper soul, or neshama. Nevertheless, pain that exists on the revealed nefesh level can lead us to an awareness of our neshama, our deeper soul. This is because we tend to think about our souls only during times of personal or collective distress. This same syndrome exists on the physical level, too. When we feel good, we don't think about our health, but when sickness strikes, we suddenly become intently focused on it.

This situation is neither desirable nor necessary, but it is extremely common. The Bible often expresses the notion that problems are a means not only to awaken us from spiritual slumber but also to help us reach a new awareness and even to choose a new path. When we experience the soul's pain on a superficial level, we usually seek superficial solutions. Only when the pain becomes deeper and more internal do we awaken to a more profound awareness. Then, when we are able to contemplate the fundamental realities of our existence, we may discover that we have a soul and that it would be appropriate to devote some attention to it.

The soul is not an ethereal abstraction. In general, it acts within reality and within a particular person. It seems logical to assume that the most basic, fundamental pains of the soul are caused by the obstacles in its path to self-realization. Yet its self-realization is simple but profound: the achievement of closeness to God.

Of course, this pain becomes more intense and more disturbing when we fail to accommodate our soul's yearning for the Divine, internally or in the world, and even more so when we do exactly the opposite. Any fault we display, or any sin or transgression we commit, inflicts pain on the soul. Since we aren't constantly aware of our souls – and, moreover, since our souls do not act directly, but through other channels and capacities – the soul's pain is not as obvious to us as our emotional and physical pain. We usually become aware of the pains of our soul through our nefesh and our consciousness. As a result, these pains do not usually manifest themselves in a clear way; they are concealed, and they penetrate our awareness indirectly, if at all. We can, therefore, suffer afflictions of the soul throughout most of our lives, perhaps sensing them in roundabout ways without identifying their source. At best, we may feel that something is off-kilter, but never quite understand that the source of the pain is not in our bodies, our lifestyles, or our circumstances – but in our souls.

Whether we are somewhat aware of the source of the pain or not, the result is almost always the same: we attempt to suppress it. We do many things that allow us to forget the pain of the soul within us. For if our minds are free and our hearts are open, we may begin to feel that we have a soul, and that the soul actually makes demands on us. Therefore, many of us feel the need to keep ourselves busy or entertained in order to avoid an encounter with our soul. We are fearful of discovering it, but even more so, we fear the demands it may make on us.

At times, we are able to escape this complex cycle in our lives – specifically, when we reach a profoundly low point, which leaves us shaken and leads us toward change. Occasionally, inner healing, of which we are not completely conscious, occurs and causes us to begin listening to our soul. Sometimes, people who had been running away from themselves for a long time become suddenly ready to accept the more lofty aspects within themselves, despite the fact that this is an extremely difficult thing to do. Very rarely, an inner revolution may occur, a sort of revelation, when the doors of the soul open clearly before us. In such a case, we feel enlightened and are able to make meaningful changes in our lives with complete clarity of mind.

It can happen that someone in perfect mental and physical health – even someone who observes the commandments – has absolutely no awareness whatsoever of the soul within. This situation is known as "dullness of the heart," *timtum halev*. Dullness of the heart has nothing to do with intellectual awareness or capability. Rather, it is a profound sense that the soul's light has completely dimmed. Dullness of the heart occurs specifically when someone is involved in holy matters that are meant to awaken the soul, and reveal it, but no such feeling arises. There is no experience of elevation of the soul at times of supposed spiritual ascent, nor is there sorrow at times of spiritual regression.

This phenomenon, which can befall people at various stages of their lives or throughout their lives, is due to an ailment of the soul, but the true meaning of dullness of the heart is a kind of impermeability related specifically to the neshama aspect of the soul, meaning that in matters related to the soul, every kind of feeling or awakening seems nonexistent. A person suffering from dullness of the heart may respond to all sorts of external stimuli: desires, aversions, fears. But in matters of the soul, there is a barrier that makes it impossible for the soul to manifest itself.

The concealment, or apparent disappearance, of the soul takes on other forms that are not always fully grasped. People often attempt to seek physiological or psychological explanations for them. This phenomenon is incredibly common but also extremely painful, and – although it is often associated with depression – there are really no ready cures for this dullness of the soul.

As we have seen, our souls can feel all kinds of pain in the context of our life experiences. But the soul suffers additional pains that are not intrinsically linked to our life processes and experiences. An individual soul can also suffer the pain of the past. This includes the past within a single lifetime, as well as past incarnations. When the past is known to us, it is possible to see a coherent sequence that unites the events of our lives. About our previous incarnations, however, we seldom remember anything. Yet this past is still attached to our individual souls.

There are often transitions in our lives that seem to mean nothing. The events of the past – and even more so, the paths, growth, and scars of the past – make an indelible imprint on the soul. Personal history, status, wealth, and family background are peripheral in comparison. At times, we invent – with or without the help of psychologists – reasons for attractions, rejections, or other experiences unique to us from the annals of our particular history. Key life events can, in fact, be related to our deep past. But so can feelings that are far less significant, and either may generate our various attractions, revulsions, and fascinations, all without any obvious connection to anything within our current lives, even if they may perhaps be significant in the larger picture of the soul's experiences.

We can, in fact, carry a lot of baggage from past lives. We are not entirely aware of this baggage, and it acts within us in a concealed way that we cannot comprehend. At times, this pain becomes exposed when we experience a similar event in the present life and respond to it in a more extreme way than the current situation would warrant. This inherited suffering, which is generated in the unknown past, as well as in the immediate environment, can play a significant role in determining the direction we decide to take in life. We might, for example, end up following a path that is the continuation of a past we do not recall. (More about past lives in the chapter called "Reincarnation.")

Because these past events and experiences are usually unknown to us, we lack the wherewithal to rectify them. We can say only that we are making an effort to correct what we can in whichever way we see fit, whether we know and understand the issues or whether they are concealed. In our nightly prayers, we ask for forgiveness for sins, faults, and wrongs we have committed and that others have committed against us, and we express the intent to rectify our actions in the current incarnation and in other ones. We are meant to know only that within our own soul, there are depths that may not be exposed to us during our lifetime, but despite this concealment, their influence is felt.

Another type of pain of the soul can be called the "pain of the Divine Presence," *tza'ar haShekhina.* This pain is unrelated to our personal lives. It is the pain of the world. And since the world is filled with suffering people, near and far, if you are a sensitive person, you are likely to suffer not only from personal pain but also from pain that you are not responsible for and have no connection with. Such sensitivity is not unique to holy people or spiritual giants, but can be part of the spiritual makeup of anyone.

Most of us, however, usually react – and are possibly taught to react – more strongly to whatever is closer to us; the farther things are from us, whether geographically or emotionally, the less impact they have. The Sages taught that in the verse "All the days of the poor are wretched, but the goodhearted have a perpetual feast" (Proverbs 15:15), the poor can mean someone who possesses a high degree of sensitivity. Such people will always encounter events that will cause them to experience pain, and since the world is replete with such events, their entire lives will be suffused with sadness. Ironically, "the goodhearted have a perpetual feast" possibly describes those who are devoid of sensitivity, but who are certainly happier in this world, from the perspective of their own personal experience.

In its broad sense, "pain of the Divine Presence" includes the entire range of pain: material or spiritual, profane or holy, in every facet of the world. Along these lines, the Sages said: "When a man suffers [in the wake of his sin], what expression does the Divine Presence utter? I am distressed about My head; I am distressed about My arm."[1] The all-encompassing Existence empathizes with all pains in existence. The pain of the Divine Presence encompasses all pain welling up out of the universe from the beginning of time.

---

1. Mishna *Sanhedrin* 6:5.

As an intellectual exercise, it is not difficult to imagine the totality of the world's pain. But as long as it remains on the intellectual plane, it does not constitute an emotional experience. For this reason, many scholars speak of the expectation that when we suffer personal pain, we will comprehend and feel it as part of the cosmic pain.[2] The same principle applies to prayer. When we pray for mercy for ourselves and our loved ones, we should view our suffering (and theirs) as part of this cosmic pain, which is the pain of the Divine Presence, the pain of the collective soul of the world.

In its essence, the human mind is meant to hold more than a collection of facts; it is meant to contain information that creates attitude and feeling. When this is the case, then "he who increases knowledge increases pain" (Ecclesiastes 1:18), since such a person not only knows, but also empathizes with, the problems of others. Those who feel the pain of the Divine Presence are holy, righteous people whose sensitivity expands and deepens the more they progress in holiness. It is also possible that an ostensibly ordinary person may genuinely sense communal pain, a pain that goes beyond the experience of the self-aware soul. This pain is a particular manifestation of the soul, which, the more it reveals itself, the more it opens up recognition of the other's pain, the pain of the stranger, of the world.

As we have already learned, we don't usually clearly perceive our soul; it does send us signs, however. At times these messages are sent through the medium of pain, which is meant to be a warning sign of what is going on within the soul. At other times, these signs arrive through enlightenment, which demonstrates that there is indeed another path. We should all take these lessons to heart, no matter where they lead us, in order to rise above the realm of sensory and bodily experience alone, and to actively pursue a more lofty direction.

---

2. Ba'al Shem Tov, *Commentary on the Torah*, "Pillar of Prayer," 152.

Death

DEATH SEVERS THE connection between body and soul; when the body dies, the soul leaves it. Since the body is a physical thing that is made up of material elements, we have a good idea of what happens to it after death. But we do not have a clear idea of what happens to the soul after it leaves the body.

In many ways, not knowing where the soul goes is the most frightening part about death. However, even a living body is in some ways unknown, since it is always undergoing change. It develops and proceeds from one stage to the next, reaches a certain point of stability, and then changes again and proceeds to another stage. These changes are never as frightening as death, though – not because of the change itself, but because death is irrevocable and unknown. Sadly, the dead are not accustomed to keeping in touch with the living and telling us how they are doing, so all we have to go on are a few hypotheses, dreams, and fantasies. That it can be discussed at all is thanks to accounts of people who have had an epiphany that opened another world to them, a world beyond sensory experience.

We know that after the soul departs from the body, the body becomes a lifeless collection of material that is subsequently influenced by various natural forces. In the end, these materials are broken down to simpler components, as the Bible explains: "For you are dust, and to dust shall you return" (Genesis 3:19). Dust is the last stage of the body's decomposition.

The soul, by contrast, cannot die, since the process of change and decomposition that exists in the physical world does not exist in the spiritual realm. The life of the soul after death is completely different from when it was part of a living person. Nevertheless, many sources, from classic mythology to folktales, demonstrate that people tend to describe the soul after it leaves the body as identical to the once-living person. After death, the soul departs from the material, tangible body; nevertheless, for some reason, many of us assume it remains exactly the same as it was when it dwelled in a body, except that it has been stripped of its clothes, bones, and flesh. What remains after all this is a form that is described in many ancient and contemporary stories as a ghost.

These metaphors and fantasies can be found not only in ancient mythologies but also in various forms in the modern world, as well as in the imaginations of multitudes of people of all religions. Some imagine the Garden of Eden as a place where we receive wings and a harp, or as a tantalizing place where people are able to fulfill all their bodily desires. While all these images of life after death are the product of superficial thinking, it is easy to understand why some people imagine the Garden of Eden as, say, an eternal vacation in the South Pacific. It feels good to dream that something like that awaits us after years of toil and, often, physical and spiritual pain. What could be better than a world devoid of disease, financial problems, and fear of death – that also contains rest, tranquility, and reunion with all our already-departed relatives and loved ones?

As we have said, all of these and other imaginary after-worlds have appeared in stories and folk literature all around the world throughout the ages. They are inspired not only by a natural human desire for a soothing eternity, but – perhaps more importantly – by an inability to apprehend the nature of a spiritual reality. There is, therefore, a powerful drive to ascribe material form to all spiritual matter. If, however, we are to come to a more complete understanding of the soul as a spiritual reality, we must understand these descriptions as metaphors whose purpose is to reveal something to us about entities that are difficult to describe. Maimonides writes[1] that just as one who is deaf from birth cannot understand what a sound is, and one who is blind cannot comprehend the concept of color, one who lives entirely in the physical world is incapable of comprehending the essence of spirituality.

One of the basic points in a meaningful discussion of life after death is the question of what happens to the Self. (You will recall from the chapter titled "What Is the Soul?" that this elusive entity called the Self is the product of a partnership between the body and soul.) Much that has been written about this is based on the reality of our lives in this world. However, after death, the soul is detached from the body, so it is also disconnected from the Self of the living person, although it still carries some form of memory of the prior existence of the Self. This explains certain experiences described by those who come back to life after having experienced clinical death. It appears that, even though death severs the connection between body and soul – and, by extension, the Self – the memory, including the memory of the body, does not immediately disappear from the soul. The soul had been attached to a living body, which acted on it and was influenced by it. Inevitably, the

1. In *Shemona Perakim*, or "Eight Chapters," his introduction to Mishna *Avot*.

73

soul absorbs something of its experiences with the body, so it is incapable of suddenly parting from these experiences and ties. In the corpus of Jewish mystical literature it is said that for three days after the death of the body, the soul is still hovering close to the body, so to speak, and does not completely separate from it.[2]

In short, the soul requires some time to accustom itself to its new situation. According to a number of traditional sources, the process of separation of the soul from the body is a product of the elevation of the soul. The higher the soul ascends, the weaker its connection to the body and the world around it becomes. At the earlier stages of separation, however, the soul retains its in-body experiences and memories. The soul's ascension involves processes in which all of life's experiences are distilled into their essential spiritual elements; only after these processes are completed can the soul return to its original spiritual form. While several sources mention the notion that the soul may be taken on different paths in its journey from death to the spiritual world, depending on what the person achieved spiritually in life, it seems that all souls pass through distinct stages on this journey.

After the soul departs from the body, it undergoes a process of rectification. The first stage of this process is known in the kabbalistic literature as the "hollow of a sling." Simply put, this is the most comprehensive overview possible of our lives in this world; it is similar to the old saying that "when you die, your whole life passes before your eyes." While we are alive, our active memories usually don't include our entire life's course. There is a natural process of forgetting, meaning that even memories existing in the brain are not available to consciousness. Additionally, while we are alive, the memories in our consciousness tend to focus exclusively on certain flashpoints, whether of happiness or sorrow. In

---

2. Jerusalem Talmud, *Moed Katan*, chap. 3.

the "hollow of a sling," by contrast, the soul – which is no longer connected to the body – apprehends the whole of its former life process at once. Indeed, this stage is commonly considered a stage of punishment, but its actual purpose is to bring the soul to a state of complete awareness. The soul acquires a certain comprehension of the details of events that were forgotten or hidden during its time in this world. Because the various components of that lifetime are no longer relevant, the soul absorbs a more comprehensive sense of the entirety of its life while in the body.

Only a precious few people can actually attain this bird's-eye view of life in this world while still living in it. One such individual was King Solomon, who wrote in Ecclesiastes that old age and death render life's pleasures and achievements entirely meaningless. However, the "hollow of a sling" enables every individual soul to achieve this kind of view. Every soul that departs from this world sees its own life, and some might conclude that it was nothing but "travail and vanity" (Psalms 90:10) – hard work, mingled with sin, that was devoid of purpose.

Just as various values that had depended on physical life or social conventions become less and less significant after death, other elements that in this life may have been perceived as unimportant take on new meaning and far higher value. In this world, we often consider our past and present in accordance with pain and pleasure, success and failure, but in a retrospective view, all that actually remains are the values that belong to the realm of the absolute. These values do not fade as time passes; on the contrary, they take on deeper significance. For example, asking how much a deceased person earned or lost in the stock market becomes pointless, while asking how much good she did becomes a far more fundamental question.

The "hollow-of-a-sling" view of life, which at times can be achieved only through several repetitions of the stages described above, is capable of creating a new and complete awareness. Only when we attain a memory that involves an evaluation of our lives can we move on to the next stages of the afterlife.

Everyone goes through Gehinnom, possibly quite willingly. Gehinnom is often translated as "hell," although both the original Hebrew and common translations have myriad, not necessarily consistent, connotations. For our purposes here, let's not call it hell! The "punishments" of Gehinnom are meant to bring us to a state of purity. Throughout our lives in this world, our souls absorb life's events and are affected by them. Among these events are moments of enlightenment that the pure soul in itself would not have been able to reach had it not been connected to a body, because such experiences attach to the soul only through the kinds of tools the body can provide, such as worldly experiences. But while embodiment allows the soul to develop in ways impossible without this experience, damage is also inflicted on the soul through embodiment, which can be likened to scars left by evil. Gehinnom is the state in which all these injuries are rectified and removed from the soul. The state of the deceased can be likened to one who removes clothing that has been worn for a long time and that is torn and stained. Just as it is ridiculous to say that when a garment is laundered, it is undergoing punishment for its sins, so too, what a soul undergoes in Gehinnom should be seen not as punishment but as a cleansing.

Our Sages add that the rigors of Gehinnom are limited to a certain amount of time, but this can vary. There are individuals who have already completed the rectification of their souls, either fully or partially, in this world. There are also those who, due to the magnitude of their flaws, require more extensive, deep rectification than others. It should be noted, particularly, that the flaw created by sin is not a result of the sin alone. In this world, there are punishments meted out in accordance with the sin, but in the ethereal world, all is measured in accordance with the flaw that the sin inflicts upon the soul. Therefore, the kind of person whose soul was on a low level could have committed many crimes in a lifetime, but the soul was not excessively harmed by them. On the other hand, the commission of even a small transgression could have caused great damage to a higher soul. This is because within human life, even a lofty soul is connected with, and therefore suffers from, everything that happens to a person both materially and spiritually. This does not refer to physical phenomena, of course, since these no longer exist with a spiritual soul, but to flaws that are somehow related to sanctity, that is, actions that negate sanctity or damage the soul.

There isn't much in traditional Jewish literature that shows us what Gehinnom looks or feels like, but in the wider world of folklore and legend, there is plenty, and it is embellished with elaborate descriptions and illustrations. But while these may be successful in awakening the imagination, they cannot be taken at face value. The soul, which is spiritual in nature, cannot be seared in fire or frozen in snow, for instance, so any description should be understood as metaphor and representation, not as realistic depictions.

When a soul completes the rectification process, it goes to the Garden of Eden. Both Gehinnom and the Garden of Eden are often spoken of as locations, or worlds. They do not, however, belong to the realm of geography, or even physics. Gehinnom is a "place" only in the metaphorical, almost mathematical sense of a platform or an infrastructure of a reality to which souls relate. So the geographic or physical descriptions of Gehinnom really refer to states of being. The soul can reach a state of Gehinnom and, also, a state of Eden. Because human language and thought are confined to material metaphors and physical representations, we experience difficulty trying to comprehend these situations, let alone attributing emotional significance to them. This is why we use material imagery that is available to a person living within a body. In the Garden of Eden, the soul exists in a state of pleasure derived from the radiance of the Divine Presence. The pleasure of the soul does not relate to its existence but is connected with and attributed to the deeds done by that soul in this world. Just as every soul can have weaknesses and can sin, so does every soul have connections with realms of holiness, whether through performing a divine commandment, studying Torah, or experiencing the elation that stems from holiness. The soul can cleave to holiness as it is understood within the material world. However, in truth, we cannot comprehend the genuine sanctity to which the soul relates and connects, since it is far above the level of human understanding. Even a great person who performs the commandments with inner happiness and devotion and not merely out of obligation is limited by this material existence. As long as a soul is in a body, all of the soul's potential experience is limited by the body's receptors.

In the Garden of Eden, on the other hand, the soul is in a state in which it can sense and understand everything that happened to it in this world. Any holy act performed in the world continues to exist on a spiritual plane, and since the soul is open and receptive, it takes pleasure in the radiance of the Divine Presence, or, in other words, from the experience of everything it acquired, and was preoccupied with, in this world.

Although the soul achieves an expansion of its potential to experience pleasure or pain in these abstract areas, it also returns eventually to its original essence in a certain sense, which is a static existence. In the Garden of Eden, the soul learns and perceives anew what it understood little of in this world, and the longer it stays in the ethereal worlds, the more understanding it attains. However, the soul cannot fundamentally undergo additional changes; in other words, it cannot learn a page of Talmud, so to speak, that it never learned in this world, or observe a new divine commandment that it never observed in this world, and it is certainly incapable of repenting in the ethereal world.

Within the Garden of Eden there are different levels. And the soul, while there also, discovers higher parts within itself. This is what is called in the kabbalistic literature the "higher Garden of Eden." In order to progress to a higher level, the soul must undergo additional rectifications and modifications. The processes of rectification and removal of flaws that took place in Gehinnom purified the soul enough to enable it to achieve the experience of the lower Garden of Eden, but not enough to raise it to higher levels. This is similar to the phenomenon in our world, where processes of repentance are multileveled, and those that are sufficient for one level are insufficient for another level, just as one would not require the same level of cleanliness for a dinner plate and an operating room. The process that the soul must undergo in order to reach each successively higher level is referred to as the soul's passage through the River of Fire.[3]

All this demonstrates that the existence of the soul in the Garden of Eden is not completely perfect, neither with regard to the ultimate purpose of the world nor with regard to the purpose of that particular soul. Additionally, even when the soul experiences pleasure in the Garden of Eden, that pleasure may be inhibited by its not having completed its role in this world. Such roles will not reach completion until all the tasks allotted to that soul have been performed. In such cases, that soul needs to be reborn in the world so that it can complete the tasks it did not accomplish in its previous lifetime. Additionally, there are very great souls that have

---

3. *Nahar diNur* in the original Aramaic. This kabbalistic concept is first mentioned in Daniel 7:10 and subsequently in the Talmud.

already completed their tasks but still return to this world, not for their own sake, but because others are in need of their tremendous enlightenment in order to perform their own tasks.

Finally, neither Gehinnom nor the Garden of Eden provides a complete reward or punishment. When we are alive, our existence is composed of a soul and a body, and a conscious Self between the two, as we have seen. The rectifications that take place in Gehinnom and the Garden of Eden are relevant only to the soul aspect, not to the Self aspect. This is why we believe in the resurrection of the dead, which will occur at the end of days. The purpose of the resurrection of the dead is to reconstruct the connection of body and soul in a more complete manner, in which both will undergo a certain measure of rectification and enhancement, but will return, in principle, to their previous form. Only then can the great judgment take place and the true spiritual reward be given.

Reincarnation

EVERY HUMAN SOUL is given a specific role in the world. It could be said that each of us is allotted a "plot of land" in the world to "cultivate and keep" (see Genesis 2:15). Every soul is required to fulfill the unique, specific role apportioned to it; only then will it be entitled to rest. For all sorts of reasons – obstacles, delays, personal choice, failure to perceive our role – many of us do not manage to completely fulfill the soul's mission during one lifetime. A soul that has not fulfilled its role completely, and that has even harmed itself and others in the process, is sent back to the world in order to complete the task allotted to it. If it doesn't manage to finish its task the second time, it will be sent back again for as many times as it takes. This return is referred to as a reincarnation, or *gilgul*. Although usually a soul is returned to the world for the purpose of completing its unfinished task, occasionally it may be reincarnated for another reason – because either the world in general, or a specific individual, is in need of that particular soul's contribution.

A soul that returns to the world through reincarnation does not necessarily return with the same Self as before. As we have said, a Self is not a function of the soul alone; it depends on the connections between the soul and the body, and between both of these and the environment, as well as the time and place in which that soul is living. A reincarnated soul has a new body and new flesh-and-blood parents, and it lives in a different place at a different time than the previous incarnation. All these factors create a Self that is different from the original one, despite the fact that it is the very same soul as before. The entrance of the reincarnated soul into a new body therefore means a new beginning and a new life experience for it.

Most of the time, the soul does not drag its prior memories, consciousness, and knowledge along with it into the new body. All these components of the soul's last tour on earth are not evident at all. There is, however, a vague aspect of memory that accompanies the soul in all its reincarnations. Despite its vague nature, the memory of its previous incarnation gives rise to a number of influences that affect the soul in its newly embodied state, which we could call its new spiritual Self. Thus, although the newly embodied soul doesn't exactly know how it behaved in its previous incarnation, it has a tendency to complete the parts of itself that had not been completed previously. For example, a soul that did not fulfill its duties regarding Torah study and other divine commandments, or other roles and obligations in its previous incarnation, will have a strong tendency to perform specifically those acts in the new one. The newly incarnated soul may not even understand this attraction; the deeds it is attracted to may not necessarily be intuitive, given that soul's new surroundings. Similarly, the soul experiences a vague memory of other souls. Souls that were close to one another in a previous incarnation will also be attracted to one another in the new incarnation, although on a conscious level they will not understand the reason for this attraction. This is why those who were relatives in previous incarnations will feel a special connection to each other in other incarnations as well, even though at present there are no family ties between them or any other overt connection.

Events that occurred in one incarnation can influence life in another incarnation. Experiences that cannot be clearly explained in the present life may be ramifications or completions of another life. In this vein, you could suffer much pain that has no connection to your deeds or way of life in the present. A person who is born with a deformity or whose life is replete with death, loss, and so forth may believe this suffering is an inexplicable injustice, but in reality it is a way for the soul to atone for damage it caused in a previous incarnation. Even someone whose life is not filled with suffering should pray for the ability to rectify, in the present life, the damage done in previous incarnations. Such a prayer appears in many prayer books.[1]

At times a full-soul reincarnation occurs, meaning that a whole soul enters another body. But that is not always the case. Parts or components of a single soul, or different parts of several souls, may return to our world as one soul that appears to be new but whose basic components have existed before. Sometimes souls split into several parts, referred to as *nitzotzot,* sparks or shards. Each shard is an expression, a kind of clone, of one soul, and they appear in different souls that find themselves within different people. People whose souls share shards from the same source are parts of one soul, but in their present form, they are distinct individuals. When they encounter each other, unique connections may be formed between them that often cannot be

---

1. In the Bedtime *Shema.*

explained in terms of their manifested personalities. For example, a friendship based on a bonding of souls can be formed between people who are completely different from one another in every aspect of their revealed personality. It is a bond that frequently appears spontaneously with no warning or introduction but is born of an inexplicable sense of belonging. This phenomenon exists to an even greater extent among great souls of distinguished individuals, whose sparks appear within a large number of people, often throughout many generations. For example, it is written in the *Zohar* that "in every generation there is a manifestation of the soul of Moses our teacher."[2] Thus, such souls appear in every generation, not in their full intensity, but as shards within different people, each of which has some of the characteristics of that original, great soul.

Our great masters of the soul attempted to trace the earlier reincarnations of the soul in order to help people understand the unique obligations and tasks related to their particular souls at present. In the reality that is accessible to us, we can normally choose among numerous paths, and we do not always have sufficient inner clarity to guide us to the path, or paths, we are required to take. Our revealed reality has many limitations that can cause our choices to be affected by factors that have nothing to do with our true destiny. Indeed, many people choose their path according to their education and environment. However, this kind of choice is frequently erroneous and may cause us to feel, perhaps without understanding why, that we are in a place where we don't belong, that we are treading a path that is not ours.

This type of emotional distress is one of the subtle ways the soul tries to relay to us the message that, to a greater or lesser extent, we have strayed from the path that the soul wishes us to follow. We

2. *Tikkunei Zohar* 114a.

may continue to follow the path that our current consciousness prescribes to us. Or, instead, we may wander from experience to experience on life's journey. Either way, these sensations are the result of listening to the soul's veiled message about what it is meant to do in this life. However, because these messages are not obvious and have no explanation that is accessible on a conscious level, they may cause disquiet and give us a sense of emptiness or lack of fulfillment.

Listening to the soul is not an easy undertaking.

Part III

Dreams

REAMS ARE AMONG the first things we identify as distinctly spiritual experiences. It is through our senses, on the other hand, that we apprehend external reality, that is, things that act and exist outside of us. And it is clear to us that these apprehensions are external to us. So while there is plenty of confusion in distinguishing the nefesh from the Self, dreams are a different story. We perceive our dreams as their own distinct reality. We do not view our dreams as part of our Self. Furthermore, we perceive them as something different from our experiences of the outside world. This recognition of dreams as a unique state of existence should not be taken for granted, since the recognition itself is the result of self-guided observation. Small children do not distinguish dreams from other experiences in the world. Only later do they learn to define them as dreams, as distinct from reality.

On a philosophical level, the distinction between dreams and reality is not at all simple. In the opinion of some contemporary philosophers, there is no unequivocal way to differentiate them. What's more, there is no actual way to prove that our entire lives are anything other than a continuous dream. However, if we can put philosophy and theory aside, there are a few ways to distinguish the two.

One characteristic difference between dreams and reality is that dreams lack consistency. In dreams, especially long, complicated ones, there is no set structure for moving from one episode to another or from one experience to another. One of the most common dreams involves falling, but these dreams do not subsequently show the dreamer his broken bones on the ground. The same goes for dreams about flying, in which the dreamer stops at a certain height and starts walking. It could be said that all dreams are fragmented and not consistent in any way.

Another distinction is continuity. It is unusual for us to dream in continuous episodes, while in reality, the events we experience are (usually) consistent and continuous. Furthermore, dreams, unlike reality, contain all kinds of implausible elements; they include shapes, images, and events that are completely irrational. At the time of the dream itself, though, these things all seem normal.

Considering the huge number of dreams each of us experiences, not to mention the sum total of human dreams, we might wonder if there is a common component to all dreams. It appears that one characteristic can be identified: when we are awake, we have control over our thoughts. This control serves as a kind of filter that distinguishes fact from fiction and matters we wish to think about from those we do not wish to think about. But in our dreams, this control mechanism is deactivated, and this awareness does not exist. When, for example, Joseph dreamed that other sheaves were bowing down to his sheaf, or that the sun and moon and stars were bowing down to him (Genesis 37:5–9), the question of how these things could happen most probably did not cross his mind. Only later, when he woke up, could he possibly have been puzzled by this.

So the most basic control mechanism, which is absent at the time of the dream, is the distinction between reality and fantasy. For this reason, even in the most banal dream, which can seem like a normal part of life, the dreamer does not know that it is not really happening. There is, likewise, no control mechanism governing events or scenes that could never occur in real life.

Since the dawn of humanity, we humans have attempted to comprehend the meanings of dreams. There are dreams whose meaning appears to be simple, such as when the dreamer sees something he wishes for as if it were really there. This experience is reflected in the verse "It will be like a hungry one who dreams he is eating, then wakes and is still hungry, and like a thirsty one who dreams he is drinking, then wakes and is still thirsty" (Isaiah 29:8). This is why Joseph's brothers claimed that his dreams reflected his thoughts when awake; they were not blaming him for his dreams, but for the thoughts he was thinking while awake. Indeed, when the dream is clearly a reflection of matters that we think about or desire or are afraid of when awake, we do not usually need another person to interpret the dream, since the explanation is obvious, as our Sages said: "A person is shown [in a dream] only the thoughts of his heart [when he is awake]."[1]

Whether the dream appears as a repetition of something the dreamer experienced while awake or whether it appears in a more colorful, extreme way, it is still an example of a straightforward dream. On the other hand, there are dreams that people are unable to comprehend. For example, we may see things in a dream, possibly even simple, everyday things, that we have never thought

1. Talmud *Berakhot* 55b.

about before and may not have been aware of – or familiar objects in unfamiliar shapes or combinations.

The interpretation of dreams is based chiefly on the assumption that what we see in a dream is symbolic, and these symbols require explanation. Occasionally, dream interpreters – whether in biblical times (in the time of Joseph, for example) or during later historical periods, such as the time of the Talmud – interpreted dreams according to lists that enumerated symbols and their meanings. In this sense, talmudic dream-interpreters and modern-day psychoanalysts (who may receive handsome compensation for their services) are doing the very same job, even though they are not using the same dream-interpretation manual. So where do all the images, events, and scenes in the dream come from?

There are dreams in which the source of the metaphors and images is clear, such as those containing memory fragments, a duplication of details from reality that were not completely erased, or a repetition of past events or anticipated future events – for example, when we dream of placing an object in a certain place, then wake up and go look for it there, only to discover that it was just a dream. There are dreams in which hopes are visualized as reality. And there are dreams about desires. There are dreams that result from an obscure awareness of a certain physical action, such as flying or falling. And there are dreams that end when we hear some sort of noise – an alarm clock, usually. But none of these can explain the plot of the dream, or how and when it was created.

Indeed, most dream interpretations relate to some sort of climax in the dream, but they do not explain how the dream reached that point. In this regard, it could be suggested that many dreams consist of a sort of literary composition that weaves a certain plot, one that is not necessarily related to the main point of the dream. Included in this category are different types of nightmares that express our fears. These, too, often involve a complex plot that includes a certain sense of fear, whether it is obvious or obscured, presented in an intricate literary fashion. Most dreams can be included in this category. Ignoring the convoluted story line, they often repeat its fundamental preoccupation.

There are other dreams that are pure and idyllic and about lofty matters or abstract ideas. But these, too, provide a means of expression for a soul that lives on a higher plane when we are awake. In dreams of this type, people can solve problems, such as chess or math problems, that they toiled over unsuccessfully while awake. There are many stories like this in the memoirs of mathematicians and scientists. We can certainly add to this category the dreams of holy people who dream that they are in a house of study or in the company of God, where they are giving sermons or coming up with new interpretations of the Torah. Testimonies of this type of dream appear among the writings of many people, and some of those novel Torah interpretations constitute valuable material that may even be considered authoritative in an objective sense.

An entirely different type of dream, which is usually less common, is the revelatory dream. These dreams range from minor revelations – for example, when people dream about events that took place in distant lands and that they had no way of knowing about, such as the death or illness of another person – to revelations concerning plans and events of great significance that are indeed realized at a later time. This type of dream appears frequently in the Bible.

It follows that although most dreams can be explained simply as a continuation of our waking thoughts, and sometimes as reflections of thoughts that are not entirely conscious, there are other dreams whose source appears to be beyond the one who dreams them. Our Sages say there are dreams that come through an angel and dreams that come through a demon,[2] meaning that there are dreams whose source is an external spiritual force for which the dreamer serves only as a conduit. Such dreams are not necessarily holy; they can come from the Other Side, from a place of evil. The phenomenon of dreams originating in an external source is mentioned in the Bible as well, where a distinction is made between heavenly revelations in a dream, as when God describes Himself as speaking to prophets in a dream (see Numbers 12:6) and revelations that occur in wakefulness.

Furthermore, as both the Bible and the Talmud indicate, even an authentic revelation is somewhat distorted when it occurs in the form of a dream, both with regard to its clarity and to its truth. Since the dreamer is, by definition, in a specific mental state, he processes the content of his revelation in a certain way. This could be by adding details that are unconnected to the original revelation, as is expressed in the Talmud, "It is impossible to dream without idle matters,"[3] or by omitting details. In a waking revelation, things are clearer and less subject to human involvement; the revelation works like any other visual or auditory experience in reality. The prophet Jeremiah speaks of this when explaining the difference between a dreamer of dreams and a prophet receiving a prophecy.[4] Jeremiah uses a metaphor to differentiate these two types of revelations: the words of the dreamer are compared to a mixture of straw and wheat, while the prophet's waking revelation is likened to pure wheat.[5]

Even if dreams can be attributed to various extrinsic factors, they remain, in all their forms, an inner experience occurring within the nefesh. Some dreams exist solely within the lower levels

2. Talmud *Berakhot* 55b.
3. Talmud *Berakhot* 55a.
4. Jeremiah 23:28.
5. Ibid.

of the nefesh, having no obvious connection to external stimuli; others belong to parts of the nefesh related to absorbing external sensations. Some dreams take place in higher levels of the nefesh, namely, in the area of desires and aspirations, and some may even be found on the level where the nefesh creates new structures and images, some of which are prosaic and some of which are fantastic.

Only exceptional individuals who have focused and trained their nefesh extensively can reach the level where all of their dreams are clear and illuminating. This is because during sleep, we have no control over the levels of the nefesh that are active, so we may see things in our dreams that come from the dark cellars of the nefesh. But such an experience may produce an even higher revelation of the soul itself. Since the soul is of a lofty essence, it is not limited, as the body is, to matters it understands through study or that it has registered through the senses. It can reveal to us information that is distant from us either in place or time and that we would not have direct access to when conscious. Thus, some people are able to see things in their dreams that are far beyond their own reality.

A dream like Jacob's, about "a ladder set up on the earth, and the top of it reached to heaven" (Genesis 28:12), is a dramatic instance of a revelatory dream. Since it is a dream, it does not manifest itself in an abstract way, but appears in forms that the nefesh can comprehend.

The Good and Evil Inclinations

ONE OF THE greatest difficulties the human soul has to contend with is the constant struggle between the good and evil inclinations. This is not merely the subject of fascinating stories about extraordinary events in the lives of great people, or complex novels about those whose entire lives consist of such struggles. At face value, it appears that no human being is free from internal battles, which can mostly be categorized as conflicts between good and evil. Additionally, people differ from one another in their level of awareness of this issue. Some are hardly aware of their struggles at all, while others are highly aware of them, and, consequently, the story of their unfolding is a significant part of their inner lives.

Works that deal with religious and spiritual matters relate to this issue in various ways. Some relate to evil or to various temptations as nuisances originating from outside a person. Their basic assumption is that "God made man upright" (Ecclesiastes 7:29). This is to say that human beings in general are essentially good, even though "there is not a righteous man upon earth that does good and never sins" (ibid. 7:20). The assumption remains that most people, not only the perfectly righteous, follow the path of good most of the time, and if they commit evil, it is due to external circumstances or exceptional aberrations from within.

An alternative view is very different: human spiritual life is the embodiment of inner struggles, and the entire life process of the nefesh is a saga of the clash between good and evil. Indeed, there are many parables about ways to overpower the evil inclination.

Yet another perspective, such as that of Rabbi Shneur Zalman of Liadi (in his work the *Tanya*), views this struggle as equivalent to the total life process, one that includes ups and downs, victories and defeats, on both sides, and where there are seldom unequivocal resolutions.

The different approaches to understanding the struggle of inclinations within the human heart may result from different definitions of the good and evil inclinations. What, then, is the good inclination, and what is the evil inclination? In the following paragraphs, we will discover some of the themes in the primarily traditional approaches to this subject.

According to one worldview, there is a morally correct path that is straightforward and obvious. Everything that is considered a diversion from this path, no matter what the circumstances, is considered evil. This opens a question regarding the evil inclination: what causes us to do bad things when we are able to act morally? The standard answer is that acting immorally is a mistake, the result of an external obstacle or a momentary or ongoing submission to a powerful attraction that causes us to depart from our chosen direction.

This approach is not just an abstract view but a framework for practical guidance. If we persist in following the correct way and don't attempt to find shortcuts or occupy ourselves with pursuits that we shouldn't involve ourselves in, we are guaranteed to continue on the path of good, and our struggle with the evil inclination will be minimal. This is the source of the general advice to follow the middle road, also called the "golden mean" by many masters of *mussar*, the literature of Jewish character refinement. Any departure from this path, whether in actions or thoughts, is perceived to be dangerous or even bad. The following verse from Proverbs may be read in this light: "Do not give me poverty or wealth; feed me my allotted bread" (Proverbs 30:8). The pressure of poverty may provoke a person to do negative things. In the words of Scripture: "Lest I become poor and steal" (ibid. 30:9). Although justification can be found for these acts, they are still morally problematic. On the other hand, wealth not only opens many possibilities but fosters excessive pride, which can also lead to evil. In the words of Scripture: "Lest I be sated and blaspheme, and say: Who is the Lord?" (ibid.). Consequently, we are better off on a middle road, since that is where the probability of committing evil is the least.

This perception is not limited to the material aspects of life but to development of the nefesh and character traits. For example, the moral approach of Maimonides determines that we should not be extreme with regard to any characteristic of the nefesh, since the extreme may be bad, whether in its own right or because it will serve as a foundation for evil that will appear later on. This philosophy may also be relevant to our intellectual understanding, such that even if we are all ignoramuses, we should nevertheless not strive to be excessively wise. Taking this idea itself to an extreme, King Solomon, who authored the book of Ecclesiastes, is not satisfied with advising, "Do not be overly wicked" (Ecclesiastes 7:17), but also says, "Do not be overly righteous" (ibid., 16). Each of these extremes is, itself, an invitation to do evil.

On another level, this conception of good and evil parallels our physical characteristics. Because of our physical nature, we can exist only in certain places and in conditions that support the needs of our bodies. Temperatures that are above or below a narrow range won't work for us. If temperatures are too high or too low, we will suffer anything from mild discomfort to extreme pain and even death. Our sensory organs, and through them, the perception of sounds, sights, and specific sensations of pain or pleasure, have a circumscribed range beyond which we can perceive nothing at all. We can, therefore, maintain overall health only within a specific, limited range of conditions and stimuli, outside of which lies danger or oblivion. It follows that the middle road, both in body and in soul, is not merely pleasing but also right and good. The good path is like a straight line leading us safely from one point to another, while the evil inclination is a general term for anything that causes us to depart from this line. The evil inclination is, therefore, perceived as the common denominator of all that is abnormal.

Basic human nature is perceived here as essentially good and healthy, while every departure from it is considered symptomatic of an illness, which, like a physical illness, is sometimes caused by external factors that are beyond our control, and at other times stem from a weakness, inborn or otherwise, in our normal functioning. But even those who believe that mankind is basically morally upright and well adjusted are aware that various obstacles stand in its way. At one extreme is curiosity, which leads us to places where we shouldn't go, and at the other is laziness, which prevents us from doing what we should. Temptations also arise from time to time. These are essentially normal components of human nature that sometimes, for one reason or another, become stronger than usual, which allows us to diverge from the straight and narrow path. But the natural path of a complete, healthy person is the good inclination, while the evil inclination in all its forms consists of the entire range of possible flaws.

It follows from this philosophy that if humankind were completely sound in both body and soul, and if we lived in a world mostly devoid of problems, that in itself would be the definition of "what is right and good," akin to man's existence in the Garden of Eden when we were still unsullied by sin and in complete equilibrium with our environment.

This description of the human personality, which sometimes serves as a basis for education, is optimistic and creates a sense of complacency. Most of us are simply not built like this. Our personal experiences are far less tranquil. For most of us, the struggle with inclinations is not a rare occurrence but is descriptive of our entire inner life. And not only people with spiritually elevated souls fight the temptations of the evil inclination while striving to reach heights of sanctity; these struggles are experienced daily by almost everyone, regardless of moral or religious character. Such struggles are also not a function of age or social status. They may appear even at a very tender age in various forms, and despite the changes we undergo later in life, along with changes in our inclinations, it seems that they continue to exist even in old age, sometimes until our final moments.

Consequently, alongside the above descriptions of evil and the evil inclination as marginal phenomena that only incidentally find themselves in the area of normative life, there are characterizations that paint a completely different picture. As early as the book of Genesis, the Bible offers a markedly pessimistic summary of the human condition: "For the inclination of a man's heart is evil from his youth" (Genesis 8:21). From here, it goes on to describe an existence characterized by struggles with the evil inclination and discussions of these struggles. Our Sages ask an interesting question: At what point does the evil inclination enter a person?

Does a fetus have an evil inclination? Is it activated immediately at birth, or later on? Jewish literature contains many discussions on the evil inclination and descriptions of its manifold facets. The Talmud, for example, states that "the evil inclination has seven names"[1] and describes the tremendous difficulty involved in the battle against it, as our Sages say: "A person's [evil] inclination overcomes him daily and seeks to kill him, as it is stated: "The wicked watches the righteous and seeks to kill him, and if not for the Holy One, blessed be He, Who assists [him], he would not overcome it" (Psalms 37:32).[2] This view is certainly not optimistic, but this theme is abundant in the sources.

In general, we can divide the evil inclination into three main categories: desires of the human body, desires having to do with character traits and other aspirations that are not physical, and the drive to do evil for its own sake.

PHYSICAL NEEDS AND DESIRES

The first type of evil inclination, which is frequently perceived as the central one, because it is present within us all, is made up of desires that are essentially bodily impulses. The human body is in essence no different from the bodies of animals, so that most human desires and passions are not necessarily related to the human condition and are not unique to it. Instead, they are intrinsic to the makeup of the body. The body has objective needs, such as eating, drinking, and sleeping, as well as physical systems that signal periodically that these needs must be met. We can fulfill these needs minimally, but there is a limit beyond which life is no longer possible, so we can't ignore these needs and continue to live, even if we may wish to ignore them.

---

1. Talmud *Sukka* 52a.
2. Ibid.

Various worldviews – and even some schools of morality within Judaism – assert that the very existence of the body is the source of evil. But physical needs, which are part of our basic, natural makeup, cannot truly be defined as evil. The evil inclination can be described as a deviation from the normal process of satisfying our needs and desires, resulting in damage to both body and soul.

Our natural inclinations and desires are extremely powerful. Their power is generated by the interaction between the physical need and the spiritual/emotional aspect associated with it. It is evident from observation that the purely physical part of these desires is much smaller, both quantitatively and qualitatively, than the emotion that accompanies them. Animals do not fulfill their inclinations unless a physical need arises, and when they reach satiation, they stop. Human beings, on the other hand, also have a nefesh that has its own needs, and the human nefesh can awaken aspirations and desires that do not come from a physical need but are part of the human capacity to think and imagine. This is why these desires are capable of growing, becoming complex and even distorted. Unlike animals, who eat only when they are hungry, human beings are capable not only of imagining food but of awakening within themselves an appetite for a lunch that will not be served for another three days or even months later. Human thinking, therefore, creates a great expanse for material desire and causes it to loom large in our inner world.

The differences among people with regard to their characters, their habits, and their education are also reflected in how much room they give their various passions. For some people, eating has no emotional connection to memories from the past, while others devote long hours of thought and preparation to the meals they are about to eat or to recollections of past culinary experiences. The same goes for other desires, some of which loom larger within the nefesh than in reality, whether in dreams, yearnings, or memories. In all cases, the desire originates in the physical, material side, which is essentially limited, but it extends from there to the spiritual side, where it can expand and grow endlessly.

Indeed, the human nefesh is not satisfied with the fulfillment of its needs at the most basic level. In every culture, the same objects of desire that are fundamentally simple become more and more complicated. Again, taking the culinary element as an example, people do not eat just to live; eating becomes a meal, then a festive meal, then a feast. People are constantly creating new ways of fulfilling a single basic need. A gourmet meal is not merely a few basic foods eaten absentmindedly, but complex structures in which a great deal of creativity is invested and about which many books have been, and continue to be, written. Discussions are conducted about such meals before their preparation and afterward, and much time and money is invested in them. The nefesh empowers, increases, and develops the basic physical need for satisfying the body's deficiency and adds a component of pleasure at ever-increasing levels of intensity.

Add to this the human inclination to decadence, and we not only develop an entire culture of food, but we arouse and intensify senses by using additional items. Spices, for instance, have nothing to do with satisfying basic needs. Spices, by nature, intensify the desire to eat. The greater the number and variety of spices in use – and a person may even need training to fully appreciate them – the more decadence. In any case, the types of garnishes, spices, and condiments continue to abound in our kitchens and eateries until a skyscraper of activity is constructed atop a simple, elemental human need – to the point where we are no longer eating to live, but, instead, we are living to eat.

In general, we can identify three levels within the natural inclinations. The first level is that of necessity and inevitability. A desire for food or sleep may be extreme for a person who is collapsing from hunger or exhaustion, and satisfying this need is clearly necessary. The second level is that which is necessary for the body to some extent. Whether they do so because of personal habit or societal norms, most people eat, and some sleep, more than they need to in order to survive. Obviously, a distinction should be made between satisfying vital needs and indulging in a lifestyle of overspending and luxury. The third level is about indulging a need or desire far beyond providing what is lacking, moving into addictive or dysfunctional behavior. Washing dirty hands is necessary, but doing it twenty times an hour indicates a specific disorder. In addition to obsessive actions, there are also obsessive thoughts. The unhealthy part of any inclination – that is, the part that is not its essence – is the evil inclination.

It is more difficult for us to discern what the good inclination, or "conquering" the [evil] inclination, consists of. This is because if we develop the ability or the desire within our soul to avoid satisfying basic needs of the body and soul, we may risk endangering our own existence. For example, while there are people who eat more than necessary, who focus on food and think about it excessively, there are also those who distance themselves from food. Frequently, this does not reflect good character traits and restraint, but is characteristic of an illness. In general, however, an approach of moderation indicates some level of functioning of the good inclination, whose main purpose is to satisfy natural needs without devoting too much time to thinking about them, as indicated by the verse "The righteous one eats to the satisfying of his desire, but the belly of the wicked shall lack" (Proverbs 13:25).

There are other inclinations that originate in the body and its desires, and despite the fact that they are not critical to existence, they are important. Sexual desire is not vital to an individual's existence, but it is critical for maintaining the continuity of humankind. The same is true of other urges, such as the need for rest. The question is, to what extent is the inclination necessary and unavoidable, what are its reasonable proportions, and what should be considered excessive?

NON-PHYSICAL INCLINATIONS

There are many inclinations that have nothing to do with the needs and desires of the body, but are spiritual impulses. Some of these non-physical desires exist in animals as well. These inclinations may indeed be manifested in material outcomes, but there is an abstract aspect that is not physical in itself, nor is there desire for wrongdoing. Examples are a longing for things like prestige or money, or the existence of feelings such as jealousy.

Some inclinations are desires of the soul. These are fleeting for some, but become intense and life-transforming for others. One of these is the basic desire for knowledge. This isn't referring to what drives people to spend their time at school in order to train to work in a certain area, since there is often no component of desire or passion in such activity, which is often performed under duress. Rather, we are talking about the desire for knowledge for its own sake and not the desire for knowledge to fulfill any kind of need. The desire to know, itself, does not have a predetermined moral value; there are people whose thirst for knowledge will lead them to holy concerns, while others may dedicate their lives to accumulating more and more knowledge about the physical world and everything it contains. Sometimes the desire to know is focused on unimportant matters, such as soccer scores in the previous century, or even on matters that are clearly nefarious, whether in order to utilize the information or merely to enjoy the evil feeling accompanying such knowledge. In fact, there is an element of curiosity that exists to some extent within every one of us, and such curiosity can turn into an obsession, whether it is for beauty, music, games, or many other things. These desires or inclinations are clearly neither physical, nor, for the most part, evil.

There are certain worldviews that see a perfect dichotomy between good and bad character traits, where bad character traits and any desire for them is like the evil inclination, which we are obligated to fight. On the other hand, there are good character traits, and the mere desire for them is already considered a manifestation of the good inclination. In Judaism, however, this division is not complete or unequivocal; on the contrary, the more profound approaches within our tradition entirely reject the concepts of "good character traits" and "bad character traits." Even jealousy, desire, and honor-seeking, each of which the Sages said "remove a person from the world,"[3] cannot be categorically censured, since they can actually be a cause for good. For example, it is said that "jealousy among the teachers increases wisdom."[4] In a similar vein, the Sages discussed the extent to which a person is permitted to possess the trait of pride, which can be positive in the appropriate context.[5]

Conversely, even with regard to character traits that are usually viewed as wholly positive, a strong desire may exist that not only defines our course in life, but may even draw us into addiction. Such a phenomenon can occur with the desire for music or beauty as well, which can go beyond all limits and become an inner compulsion that has the power to distort other needs and desires. This phenomenon is even clearer in the case of attributes that are considered less desirable, and which may be as strong as a physical desire, such as the desire for money. This desire can be

---

3. Mishna *Avot* 4:21.
4. Talmud *Bava Batra* 21a.
5. Talmud *Sota* 5a.

expressed in a moderate way by someone who is truly lacking, but it can also become an inclination that stands on its own, unrelated to the need for money or the ability to spend it. It becomes all-consuming for those who desire it, because they want to acquire more money than they need, and more than they can spend. Yet this does not stop them from acquiring still more of it. Similarly, jealousy and the pursuit of prestige are traits that can reach murky depths that do not merely reflect a darkness of the nefesh, but become a fertile ground for evil thoughts and repugnant fantasies to take root, and lead people to commit terrible acts.

However, as above, these inclinations in themselves are not necessarily bad. A distinction should be made between desire and the directions it causes a person to go in, and the ways in which it is expressed and realized. There are people for whom these ambitions can take on noble forms. For example, one who feels honored when in the company of sages or righteous people, or one who is envious of the sanctity of the angels, may achieve an elevation of the nefesh rather than a descent. The same is true for other desires that are considered worse or inferior to these, such as stinginess or hatred of other people. It all depends on the object they are applied to. The paradoxical verse "You who love the Lord, hate evil!" (Psalms 97:10) implies that there can be positive hatred, and also that such hatred is a requirement addressed specifically to those whose nature contradicts it. They are encouraged to cultivate it because it is necessary in the reality of this world. Even the trait of stinginess appears in many forms that sometimes differ from one another only in their degree or direction; at times they are even praiseworthy, such as when they are expressed in frugality and moderation.

In general, many of the non-physical desires of the nefesh cannot be judged by the names that were given to them, whether they are neutral or negative. The various desires of the nefesh can be viewed simply as tools in our hands. Most tools in the world have more than one use; even the tools that seem the most innocent can be used for aggressive, negative purposes, just as tools whose normal use is negative can be utilized for positive goals. Of course, there are tools, such as pots or dishes, that are easier to use for positive purposes, or at the very least, purposes that do not distort the nefesh, but even tools that embody some degree of danger, such as knives, do not have to be employed as weapons but may be used simply for slicing vegetables. Similarly, dynamite can be used for manufacturing bombs and also for building roads.

We should relate to the traits of the nefesh in the same way. There are traits that are normally positive and others that are commonly negative. However, in the broader picture of our aspirations and desires, distinguishing between good and evil does not entail identifying and sorting the needs and aspirations according to some sort of predefined method; what is important is the intelligent use of these desires in any given situation. Generosity and tolerance, generally considered positive traits, often express as weakness or the inability to set limits. Similarly, excessive generosity can lead to a variety of negative traits within its recipients, such as parasitism, lack of consideration for others, or unlimited desire, while excessive tolerance can express lack of interest or even apathy, and thus serve as a backdrop for the development of many types of evil.

It follows that there are no simple, unequivocal parameters with which to evaluate the results of our actions or even the urges that lead to them. For better or worse, there are no colors or shapes in our souls that enable us to distinguish between these urges easily. The complexity of human existence weaves intricate patterns within which we cannot immediately or easily differentiate between good and evil, between the summit and the abyss.

All of this is important not only with regard to educating children but for relating to people in general. Parents and teachers, preachers and authors, frequently take the easy path by sorting the content of the human soul into simple, unambiguous categories. However, these divisions are not necessarily true to real life. The statement of the prophet Jeremiah that "the heart is deceitful above all things, and it is exceedingly weak; who can know it?" (Jeremiah 17:9) is much closer to the truth. The evil inclination is not an independently defined unit but part of the entire physical-spiritual package that is the human being. What is common among the inclinations is that they are inclinations, meaning that their primary source is not in the mind but in a certain urge that exists within us. In order for it to be realized, this urge indeed needs the tools of the nefesh, such as the power of thought and action, but the dominant, activating power will always be an inclination, an attraction or longing of the nefesh. It is true that, in practice, our rational minds may be capable of overriding the inclination and leading us in a certain direction, but at its root, that same primary, primal, powerful inclinational element still exists.

Some scholars relate to the ensemble of human inclinations as our "animal soul," meaning the component of human beings that makes us part of the animal world, a creature among creatures. This definition is more accurate than the definition of inclinations as "good" or "evil," since almost all human inclinations, as above, are morally neutral, neither intrinsically good nor bad. Their tendency toward good or evil depends to a great extent on the way they are managed and applied. This also explains why the general definition of inclinations (including those that we share with animals) doesn't include only desires that every animal is capable of fulfilling. Some human inclinations are typically human in the sense that they do not exist among animals, at least not on the same level. But even assuming that they are unique to human beings, even when these inclinations take on abstract and sublime forms, they are still part of the manifestation of man as a biological creature. The inclination that motivates human beings to acquire knowledge or create objects of beauty is essentially no different from the inclination that motivates birds to fly. Just as the bird wants to fly because it has wings, so do we want to use our brains because we have them.

Inclinations, especially ones that lack material parameters, are unlimited, so they can become infinitely powerful and develop in different directions. Despite their neutral essence, they are like vigorous streams bursting out of the depths. When we lose control of them, they can become as destructive as boiling lava, but when they are limited and directed to good ends, they are powerful forces that create good in the world. Not only that: while animals have powerful instinctual systems that drive their inclinations and also limit them, human beings almost completely lack such systems and we must construct them on our own, based on the foundations given to us through education, society, and acquired knowledge. This means that the human mechanism that attempts to limit the inclination is what creates these struggles.

The driving force behind each inclination is a primal power that is not a product of organized thought or conscious desires but an independent entity. However, both the general tendency of the inclination, as well as the actual use to which it is put, are built on the power of the human being to regulate these inclinations and control them. The rational parts of the human being are merely tools for implementation, not a basic part of our makeup, since, in its essence, the "good inclination" is not an intense desire whose weight is equal to that of the other inclinations but rather a structure, an alignment that we must maintain as we attempt to remain within the limits it sets out. This is why mankind's struggle with his inclination is always a difficult battle.

PURE EVIL

In addition to the many different inclinations, there is one that is apparently unique to human beings, which, while often called the "evil inclination," is less prevalent than the other inclinations and is not always as powerful as they are. This is the desire to do wrong, not for any particular reason such as enjoyment or benefit, but for the sake of doing evil. The human nefesh contains an attraction to evil that at times completely contradicts logic and even the desire for pleasure. Such a tendency can appear even within a young child, who may cause harm just because it is forbidden. Among adults, especially those with developed minds, this tendency toward evil can be extremely destructive. At times people can even rationalize this desire, just as they can rationalize other inclinations. In Jewish literature this inclination is called Amalek. It can manifest in insignificant, material matters but may also take on literary or even philosophical forms.

However, unlike the other aspects of the nefesh, which can be channeled and refined, this aspect of it is an entity of pure evil and is incorrigible. This is why the Torah commands us to eradicate it completely. Thankfully, "Amalek" as a social phenomenon is not the driving force in the world, although it does exist. What is more prevalent is what is called poetically "the seed of Amalek." This refers to the small seed of evil that can exist in the soul of any person, which is like a poison that interferes with everything within and can even lead to our demise. The only way to rectify matters is to utterly eradicate it by using the sublime powers of the soul. This can be accomplished only by means of prayer and requests for divine assistance.

Free Will

F

REE WILL IS a complex topic with all sorts of philosophical, theological, and scientific dimensions. But boiled down to its
basic assumption, free will is the notion that we human beings are
endowed with the freedom to choose our destiny.

The opposite of free will is determinism (or causality/cause
and effect), and from this outlook, everything has a cause, and
the cause has a cause, creating a continuous chain of cause and
effect. Therefore, we could say that every occurrence, whether in
the physical world or in our thoughts, is the result of everything
that preceded it. While this is undeniably true, there is still room
within this point of view to accommodate free will. For example,
our subjective sense tells us that we are capable of choosing. Of
course, there are limits to this ability, but we are aware of them,
so they do not negate the perception of the ability to choose
completely. But the best case that can be made for free will is our
ability to cast doubt upon it. If there is no free will, then there
is no freedom of thought either, since every thought, as well
as every observation, understanding, or perception, is the net

result of all the causes that preceded it. Doubt and skepticism must, therefore, assume the existence of free will, which enables us to choose not only between good and evil but between truth and untruth.

Nevertheless, we do live in a world of causality in which events materialize, not at will, but because of other forces. In the case of inanimate objects or non-sentient creatures such as plants, the active forces are physical and chemical. In the case of creatures who possess consciousness, such as humans, the active forces are determined not necessarily by choice but by conditioning – whether hereditary, cultural, or educational. Within the forces that are active in reality as we perceive it, there is an entire system of causality that determines the course of everything in creation, from the movements of the celestial bodies to the tiny movements of leaves or bacteria. And everything is, as a matter of necessity, part of this causal system in which one thing leads to another. Whether the causes and effects derive from natural forces or divine decree, it does appear to preclude the possibility that humankind, or anyone or anything else, ever has the option to make choices about their destiny.

Furthermore, causality does not relate exclusively to the elements of the material world. Scripture and Kabbalah both teach us that even heavenly beings, despite having far more power and understanding than humans, in certain respects behave in a manner similar to animals and objects. An angel may be more powerful than a human being, but an angel does not have any more free will than a steamroller. Although governed by a different set of rules and forces than those at work in the material world, these beings are still subject to the constraints of determinism. An angel cannot change his role, just as a pine tree cannot turn into a date palm; they are also confined to their respective modes of existence, to the same laws that guide existence in its entirety.

Therefore, the universe in its broadest sense, including both material and spiritual realms, is a system whose processes are limited and whose movements are predetermined, following a fixed plan.

So where does free will fit into all of this?

This question gives rise to another question that is both philosophical and quintessentially religious: is the chain of causality affected solely by the causes that created it, or can the decisions and actions of human beings alter it? This problem cannot be solved by means of the mind alone. It is a matter of faith: do we believe that the world has a purpose?

In the entire expanse of the universe, there are only two beings that have free will: God above and humans beings below. The divine spark within man is the spark of free will. Mankind is a unique presence in the world in the sense that we have the ability to move within reality and shape it in accordance with our wishes, that is, in accordance with our conscious or unconscious decisions. A storm, a cloud, and a flame all have a determined, defined structure; ants and grasshoppers have a fixed route. But only human beings can make decisions that can change these systems. Mankind's possibilities are limited from a physical and spiritual point of view, but his ability to choose is unlimited.

In the account of creation, the Bible relates: "God blessed them, and God said to them: Be fruitful, and multiply, and replenish the earth, and subdue it; and have dominion over the fish of the sea, and over the fowl of the air, and over every living thing that creeps upon the earth" (Genesis 1:28). This promise of human control of the world is not immediately realizable, because any one individual may not be able to utilize all the available possibilities. Similarly, the human race as a whole needs a sufficient amount of time, as well as the appropriate conditions, to discover the possibilities embodied in this freedom. Mankind's free will not only gives us the possibility to go beyond the fixed path determined by time and place, but also enables us to harness various forces, together or in opposition to one another, in order to create changes in the material and spiritual worlds. This is why human beings are capable of creating poems and songs, even though we do not have the voice of a nightingale, while no nightingale is capable of composing even the simplest rhyme. The psalmist, with a mixture of thanks and wonder, declares: "You have made him but a little lower than God....You have put all things under his feet" (Psalms 8:5–6). In his ability to truly change and be changed, man is comparable to God alone.

Free will gives mankind the ability to choose, but since it is a freedom, it doesn't dictate what to choose. This is why people are capable of performing both sublime acts and abhorrent crimes. Mankind's ability to rise above mountains and angels is the same capability that permits us to fall to the most profound depths, to be more putrid than a carcass and more poisonous than a snake. Since the essence of freedom is the possibility to move in opposing directions, free will necessarily includes the ability to choose evil. So human error is the result of a bad choice. Although it is not always intentional, it invariably stems from free will. It follows that the commission of sins and transgressions, as well as the fulfillment of commandments and the performance of good deeds, result from that same freedom.

Although free will is absolute in principle, and the decision to turn left or right, to move up or down, depends on man alone, in reality there are constraints. If we must choose between two paths, one of which is strewn with rocks, mud, and other hazards, while the other is pleasant and convenient, our decision will be biased. However, free will includes an override option. Many who gave their lives for the sanctity of God's name faced an unbalanced choice – but it seems that even when their bodies could not withstand the ordeal, their spirits, meaning their inner ability to choose, remained unharmed.

Of course, despite the existence of free will, it is possible to force people into slavery or to cause them to make declarations that they do not believe in, but this does not damage their free will in its purest form. Only in rare cases, the understanding of which requires additional study, can it be said that God takes away an individual's free will. And since free will is the essence of man's soul, when it is taken away from him, he ceases to be human and becomes a mere object, an earthenware shard.

Because mankind has the freedom to choose, it would seem that even God can only ask us to behave in a certain way but not force us. Consider the following verse: "I have set before you life and death, the blessing and the curse; therefore choose life that you may live" (Deuteronomy 30:19). Such a choice should be obvious, but even with such a simple decision we are still implored to "therefore choose life."

Mankind's capacity to choose freely, then, is the manifestation of the Divine in the human being, since only we humans can extricate ourselves from the chain of causality.

Dreams, Plans, and Aspirations

WHILE WE LIVE in the present, we can remember the past. The future, on the other hand, is completely unknown, but that doesn't stop us from thinking about it. There are three kinds of thoughts that we have about the future: dreams, plans, and aspirations. Whether the future seems secure and promising or whether it is a source of fear and worry, these will always be the ways in which we relate to it.

DREAMS

From childhood, dreaming, or imagining, is the first apprehension of the future that we develop. Dreams in this context are, of course, conscious, usually waking dreams, which include imaginings, expectations, or ideas that we use to picture our future. Some are short and fragmented, such as "I want to be X," but some are long, complex ideations of what we want to happen in the future.

Some of these conscious dreams are simple and realistic, while others are highly imaginative and disconnected from reality. A young child can talk about aspirations for the future very concisely, for example, "When I am big, I will be a policeman," or "When I grow up, I will be a firefighter." This is an elaboration of a dream, or wish, with no imaginative component, and it may very well come true. But a child, and even more so, an adult, may also harbor grandiose dreams whose chances of being realized are far smaller, or even non-existent, such as "I will be a millionaire," "I will be a famous author," or "I will be a king," yet this does not prevent the dreamer from dreaming them. There are dreamers who express with simplicity a future desire or wish, while others spend a significant amount of time every day imagining the future. There are others whose dreams about the future become almost a replacement for real life and, at times, actually disrupt daily life. And just as there are people who dream of every possible topic in the world, from dreams about a certain life course to dreams about love and so on, there are dreamers who dream not only about themselves but also about a group of people, even an entire nation.

The common denominator of the innumerable dreams that we have about the future is their detachment from reality. They are wishes, which normally do not create anything but a personal experience for the dreamer; in most cases, they do not involve ways of bringing the wishes to fruition. Indeed, we can continue to dream the very same dream for years, expressing desires and wishes, and nothing more. In this sense, dreams about the future are expressions of certain aspects of the soul's wishes. While most dreams of ordinary people – whether they are morally neutral or about inappropriate, negative acts – are expressions of the nefesh in the most simple, lowest sense, dreams can also reflect higher levels of the soul. Thus, just as one person may dream of being extremely wealthy, another may dream of becoming a great Torah scholar or a righteous, holy person.

Moreover, conscious dreams, which are expressions of the conscious mind, are continually created and changing, just as consciousness is continually evolving. And since these dreams are connected to our consciousness, there is clearly a difference between the dreams of a child and the dreams of an adult, depending on the individual's evolving wishes and knowledge of the world.

PLANS

Another type of contemplation of the future comes in the form of plans. Plans, too, are structures relating to what might occur or what we desire to occur in the future. However, unlike dreams, plans involve seeking or constructing modes of implementation. Plans, especially detailed plans, are usually made at mature ages. However, even children, whose ability to manage or calculate matters is more limited, can have real plans that include at least some kind of outline for implementation, and at times even more than that. In any case, whether the plan is "We will play soccer the day after tomorrow," "I want to be an engineer," or "I want to pay my debts to the bank," a plan, as opposed to a dream, is meant to be implemented.

A dream turns into a plan when a layer of practicality and a list of actions are added. The transition from a dream to a plan removes the matter from the realm of the nefesh and brings it closer to the real world. While a dream can provide a feeling of satisfaction, a plan requires a certain degree of effort and action. A plan is therefore an act of creating the future (although the future can, of course, disrupt or destroy plans). As with dreams, the content of plans can vary dramatically from person to person. A significant part of our lives is spent creating and realizing plans, no matter whether they are short term or long term, and no matter what the content. Even an expression such as "I want to go to the grocery store" is a kind of plan that requires action and implementation. But a plan such as "I am going to medical school" or "I want to build a factory" is more complex and requires sustained attention to the relevant modes of implementation.

When King Solomon said, "Many plans are in a man's heart" (Proverbs 19:21), he was referring to the myriad plans people make. All plans are a tapestry woven from the hopes of the nefesh and the reality of the world. What might seem to be a working plan could turn out to be an almost unobtainable dream. And since each of us has limited possibilities in this world, certain plans may not be realized at all. Willpower, on the one hand, and external conditions, on the other, are important factors that will lead either to the plan's implementation or to its stagnation in the dream stage. The scope of the plans and their practicality also play an important role.

It is sad, but true, that some people make very few plans. If life dishes up harsh difficulties or financial or emotional distress, then all energy is channeled into survival, leaving little time to think about the future.

ASPIRATIONS

Every working plan or outline for action includes a fundamental goal or an overall desire that underpins dreams and plans. In order to understand this fundamental goal, we must ask, "What does the planner aspire to in principle?" Most of us have more than one aspiration; some have many. We tend to classify them according to the importance we attribute to each one.

Aspirations can be nothing more than the sum total of our desires, but they can also consist of higher yearnings and even elements associated with the foundations of the soul. When we create plans, we aspire to specific goals that our plans are meant to promote. These aspirations could be for prestige, power, fame, or money, but could also be for tranquility, respite, or security in old age, or for accomplishing great things. But even if we lack significant aspirations, it doesn't mean we aren't thinking about the future; it only indicates that our plans for the future are not focused on specific values, so they tend to have limited scope.

Our aspirations do not always derive from clear thinking or profound reflection. At times, we build our lives – meaning our future – in a certain way because we are part of a society that defines aspirations in that way. During periods of introspection, as well as periods of distress, we are often able to understand what motivates us. For example, suppose you are planning to build as many huge buildings as possible. At a certain point, you may be asked, by yourself or by others, "Why are you doing this?" A genuine response to this question might be "Because doing so enables me to make a lot of money" or "Because I desire fame and prestige." On the other hand, the motivating factor could be the desire to create or just to do something new. In any case, the more clearly we understand our desires, the more focused and directed our plans will be. Alternatively, we may cancel or change our plans entirely when our true motivation becomes apparent. Thus, for example, the realization that our true aspiration is to acquire security for ourselves and our families may cause us, henceforth, to follow a completely different course, or to accomplish exactly what we had planned in the first place, but in a different way or by different methods.

These yearnings of the heart that appear in the form of aspirations may be low key. At other times, they may be agitated and pervasive, not allowing any respite. For example, in the case of a love of money that appears in the form of an uncontrollable passion, the verse states: "He who loves money will not be satisfied with money" (Ecclesiastes 5:9). The same goes for other desires such as prestige, control, or power, which can become an obsession that pushes aside all other concerns. The all-encompassing nature of an aspiration is sometimes especially obvious in people who have actually fulfilled their wishes, but it can also be obvious in people who are driven by desires that they are unsuccessful in satisfying.

The heart's desires are in fact the foundation of our aspirations and plans. In addition to all kinds of ordinary desires, whether noble or more self-oriented, there are desires of a baser order. Vengeance is a prime example. If vengeance against one person, a few people, or a group becomes a significant component of someone's larger plans, then years or an entire lifetime can be spent in this sad and unproductive way. Examples of this in the world of literature are *Max and Moritz*, by Wilhelm Busch, and *The Count of Monte Cristo*, by Alexandre Dumas. Hatred is another example. It can be a fleeting phenomenon or the leitmotif of a life.

Happily, the overarching desires of most people are noble, or, if not noble, at least harmless. And they develop their life's path in that direction. Such is the case for those who aspire to help people in distress. Others aspire to beauty in all its forms, whether in the visual arts, music, or literature. For these people, the desire for beauty is not merely a sensitivity or an inclination, but the driving force in their lives. For others, the desire may be to acquire knowledge, and they, too, plan and construct their lives in accordance with this desire. There are also people whose heart's desire is to worship God, and their lives are directed along paths for realizing this aspiration, perhaps by observing commandments, praying, or studying Torah. Even such abstract desires are particularized into many plans of action, all of which are directed toward the greater goal of sanctity. We can say that the entire Jewish people was given the task of performing certain acts, and, also, the overriding admonishment "[A]nd you shall be holy" (Leviticus 11:44), so that education, study, and life plans are all meant to be directed toward this end.

In general, it could be said that these overarching desires are the most stable expression of the manifestation of the soul within us. Great souls have great wishes, while small souls have small wishes; lower souls may turn to lower, even undesirable pursuits, while high souls, holy souls, will be led to discovering higher levels of the soul while realizing the overall desire of their personal lives.

Although we do not choose our own soul or the way in which it reveals itself, each one of us is capable of discovering more noble elements within ourselves. The inner work before us is to find a way to access the higher levels of our soul. Then we must cause those higher levels to be manifest within our lives.

What people search for within themselves, they will find. There are many processes that enable us to access the higher levels of our souls and also to express them to a greater or lesser extent. Some undergo a onetime or sudden epiphany, while others need a great deal of time to access these higher levels. The Sages have said that mankind is "of the dust of the ground" (Genesis 2:7), and yet we are considered to be like God, as the verse states: "I will be like the Most High" (Isaiah 14:14).[1]

Humankind is capable of going beyond the realms of speech, action, and thought to achieve a state where lofty matters become their own overriding desire.

---

1. *Shenei Luḥot HaBerit, Toldot Adam*, introduction, section 23.

Listening to the Soul

THE SOUL WITHIN us is always present and is always speaking to us, but it is usually a still, small voice that is overshadowed or silenced by many louder voices both within us and from the world around us. Our body, for example, has a powerful voice that can almost never be ignored, and it often silences the whisper of the soul.

One of the ways we can hear the voice of our soul is by disconnecting from the noises of the environment. At times, this detachment happens spontaneously – when we find ourselves alone, for instance, without anything to distract our thoughts. But in case we don't often happen to find ourselves alone with our thoughts, we can create such an environment for ourselves. In certain places, or in accordance with certain traditions, aspiring practitioners are sent off to be alone for a specific period of time, not for the experience, but in order to develop the capability of listening to their inner voice. It is said that some of the prophets would go off to the desert as a way to achieve that kind of listening. When we are surrounded by people and spend our time observing others, even if we refrain from speaking or doing anything whatsoever, we certainly do not achieve solitude.

Solitary meditation, *hitbodedut,* is one way to minimize, if not eliminate, surrounding noises. The idea is to create an internal environment in which external disturbances are neutralized. Even if you cannot find a place to meditate in seclusion, you can teach yourself to achieve the same effect even when you are not entirely alone. It is even possible to meditate in this way when lying in bed or when surrounded by people. This type of meditation, however, requires a concerted effort – and practice – to isolate and neutralize environmental interference.

It is a common misconception that the ability to disconnect in this way is an inborn trait or a unique spiritual capability. Most of us are capable, with sufficient effort, of focusing on one topic and ignoring the sights and sounds in the environment. All of us, probably, at one time or another, have been caught daydreaming and, while thus engaged, do not see or hear a thing that is happening around us. In almost every classroom, there are at least one or two students who seem always in their own world and display no connection to the reality surrounding them. Almost all of us are capable of achieving this kind of detachment if we really desire it. But this is not exactly what meditation in seclusion is about. *Hitbodedut* is a state in which we can hear our own soul to some degree. In order to do this, we must ignore not only external stimuli, but even those we create within ourselves.

The whispering voice of the soul has many facets, and it speaks of diverse matters. The soul speaks, whispers, makes comments, raises doubts, and asks questions about matters that the ostensibly all-encompassing structure of life does not address at all. Questions such as "What did I do?" "What am I doing?" "What am I planning to do?" all belong to the same category – the voice of a soul that is unhappy about where it is being led. But the longer we manage to listen, the more able we are to hear a single whisper that says, "Maybe it is possible to choose differently." Those who are good at listening to the messages this inner voice relays are able to achieve amazing changes in their lives.

The need to listen to the soul is not a luxury but a genuine necessity, both for those who already pay attention to it and those who are entirely unaware of it. As with essential vitamins whose absence does not awaken an intense desire to fill the void, but is nevertheless capable of causing weakness, disease, and even death, listening to the soul is also a vital need, even though this imperative is not keenly felt by many. The main significance of listening to the soul does not specifically relate to details, that is, performing certain actions or refraining from them. It is something more fundamental that involves finding a general direction in life.

Life's events lead people in different directions. For many, life is entirely random, while others find their way intentionally and with forethought in order to realize their plans and dreams. However, even a path that we tread through conscious choice is not necessarily the correct path for us. We can walk on a paved road overlooking a breathtaking view but still discover that we are marching energetically in the wrong direction entirely. Similarly, we may not merely survive but even flourish while treading a life path that is leading us in the wrong direction.

Listening to the soul's voice is a kind of navigation in which we face fundamental issues. When God asked man, "Where are you?" (Genesis 3:9), He was not asking for geographical information, nor was He even referring to any one point in time. He was interested in man's direction, his aspirations. And this question still stands. Every person is asked it. It is a question that relates to the essence of our lives and is meant to define our roles and direct our paths. Nevertheless, it is easy and common to ignore the intensity of the question, and the number of reasons and excuses we provide for failing to address the question, either to God or to ourselves, is infinite.

When we do reach a point where we listen to our soul, we may hear it in a number of different ways. If we reach this point following years of disconnection, after a lifetime filled with noise in which we did not hear any inner voices, we will not hear the voice within us in full clarity; it will, more likely, be heard as an almost imperceptible murmur. We might feel amazed that we have a soul at all, like someone who has a relative in a distant country whom he happens to meet after years pass with absolutely no contact, and he is awestruck over the fact that the relative is still alive. As we begin to listen with concentration to the voice of our soul, however, it gradually becomes clear. It is not always a response to our recent past or present life; at times it might cause us to recall old and forgotten experiences. But if we listen to the voice persistently, either at the time it first makes itself heard or even only later on, we will not only understand that we have a soul, but we will also begin to hear what it is saying about our current existence.

Not only the errant among us but even the righteous may live without feeling the presence of the soul. Still, there is a difference between the voice of the soul speaking to a person who dwells in the "courtyards of the Lord" (Psalms 92:14) and one who is standing at the edge of the abyss. For the former, the soul may say something like "You have done well, but why have you forgotten me?" while for the latter, it may be a great cry: "What have you done to yourself? Look where you are now!"

With our wonderful free will, we humans can choose to ignore the voice of the soul, and even make an effort to silence it. By the same token, we can choose to make far-reaching decisions based upon that voice, not only in our thoughts but in practice also.

Extraordinary or onetime events can jolt us into listening to our soul, but minor events can, too. However, the advice of the poet, "Pay attention to the soul,"[1] is a call to listen to the soul continuously, not only in the face of a rare event or at the end of life, but as an ongoing and focused inner spiritual process. When we deliberately silence the noises of life and listen, instead, to the inner voice of our soul, we can achieve the level of "a person's soul will teach him." Those who attain this exalted level may be completely different from one another in all respects, but they all have a kind of inner illumination that is visible even to others, and that shows they have been able to hear their soul. The more we are able to listen to our soul, the more its voice will affect our lives and the way we understand the world.

---

1. From the liturgical poem of the same name by Shmaya Kosson.

About the Author

RABBI ADIN EVEN-ISRAEL Steinsaltz is a teacher, philosopher, social critic, and prolific author who has been hailed by *Time* magazine as a "once-in-a-millennium scholar." His lifelong work in Jewish education earned him the Israel Prize, his country's highest honor.

Born in Jerusalem in 1937 to secular parents, Rabbi Steinsaltz studied physics and chemistry at Hebrew University. He established several experimental schools and, at the age of twenty-four, became Israel's youngest school principal.

In 1965, he began his monumental Hebrew translation and commentary on the Talmud. By 2010, all forty-four volumes were completed and in the process of translation to English, with the majority already in print as this book goes to press. The Rabbi's classic work of Kabbalah, *The Thirteen Petalled Rose*, was first published in 1980 and has been translated into eight languages. In all, Rabbi Steinsaltz has authored some sixty books and hundreds of articles on subjects ranging from zoology to theology, and he often engages in social commentary as well.

Continuing his work as a teacher and spiritual mentor, Rabbi Steinsaltz established a network of schools and educational institutions in Israel and the former Soviet Union. He has served as scholar in residence at the Woodrow Wilson Center for International Studies in Washington, D.C., and the Institute for Advanced Studies at Princeton University. His honorary degrees include doctorates from Yeshiva University, Ben-Gurion University of the Negev, Bar-Ilan University, Brandeis University, and Florida International University.

Rabbi Steinsaltz lives in Jerusalem. He and his wife have three children and many grandchildren.

Credits

Editor in Chief: Rabbi Jason Rappoport

Translator: Adina Luber

Editor: Shoshana Rotem

Proofreader: Suri Brand

Cover design: Tani Bayer

With thanks to our colleagues at Maggid Books: Matthew Miller, Rabbi Reuven Ziegler, Shira Finson, and Tomi Mager.

Other works by Rabbi Adin Even-Israel Steinsaltz
available from Maggid Books

A Dear Son to Me

Biblical Images

The Candle of God

Change and Renewal

The Essential Talmud

In the Beginning

The Long Shorter Way

My Rebbe

The Strife of the Spirit

The Sustaining Utterance

The Tales of Rabbi Nachman of Bratslav

Talks on the Parasha

Talmudic Images

Teshuvah

The Thirteen Petalled Rose

Maggid Books
The best of contemporary Jewish thought from
Koren Publishers Jerusalem Ltd.